GABRIEL DUMONT

War Leader of the Métis

BY DAN ASFAR & TIM C

FOLK
LORE
PUBLISHING

© 2003 by Folklore Publishing
First printed in 2003 10 9 8 7 6 5 4 3 2 1
Printed in Canada

The Publisher: Folklore Publishing
Website: www.folklorepublishing.com

National Library of Canada Cataloguing in Publication

Chodan, Tim, 1970–
   Gabriel Dumont: war leader of the Métis / by Tim Chodan & Dan Asfar.

   (Legends series)
   Includes bibliographical references.
   ISBN 1-894864-06-9

   1. Dumont, Gabriel, 1837–1906. 2. Red River Rebellion, 1869–1870. 3. Northwest, Canadian—History—1870–1905. 4. Métis—Canada, Western—Biography. I. Asfar, Dan, 1973– II. Title. II. Series: Legends series (Edmonton, Alta.)

FC3217.1.D84C48 2003   971.05'4'092   C2003-900646-0

Project Director: Faye Boer
Cover Image: Courtesy of Glenbow Archives, Calgary, Canada, NA-3432-2
Photography credits: Every effort has been made to accurately credit the sources of photographs. Any errors or omissions should be directed to the publisher for changes in future editions. *Photographs courtesy of* Archives of Manitoba (p. 15, N-12762; p. 148, N-9289; p. 192, N-7582); Glenbow Archives, Calgary, Canada (title page, NA-3432-2; p. 10, NA-1063-1; p. 60, NA-47-34; p. 70, NA-20.8; p. 73, NA-1829-5; p. 76, NA-1406-23; p. 89, NA-1177-1; p. 102, NA-343-1; p. 124, NA-23-3; p. 132, NA-1315-18; p. 133, NA-1494-2; p. 135, NA-1847-2; p. 171, NA-363-50; p. 175, NA-1032-3; p. 178, NA-363-48; p.185, NA-363-43;); Library of Congress (p. 212, USZ62-113198); Montana Historical Society (p. 201); National Archives of Canada (p. 36, C-47151; p. 104, PA-12197; p. 151, C-04590; p. 207, C-1897); RCMP Museum, Regina, Saskatchewan (p. 225); Saskatchewan Archives Board (p. 31, R-A3955; p. 68, R-B714; p. 85, R-A5680; p. 98, R-B714; p. 220, R-A8211; p. 226, 61-310-04); *The American West in the Nineteenth Century*, 1992 Dover Publications (p. 56).

We acknowledge the support of the Alberta Foundation for the Arts for our publishing program.

COMMITTED TO THE DEVELOPMENT OF CULTURE AND THE ARTS

PC: 5

Contents

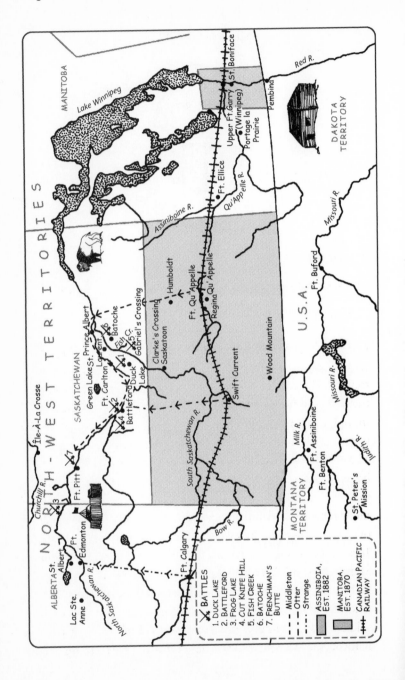

CHAPTER ONE

Origins

"Just a minute; I want to kill another Englishman."

GABRIEL DUMONT STARED DOWN the barrel of his Winchester, singling out one Canadian soldier from the throng charging forward. The grizzled Métis hunter paused long enough to note that the man running towards him had bright blond hair and moved with a barely perceptible limp. Perhaps the lopsided gait was the remnant of some boyhood accident. It might have been a broken bone that didn't set right after a mishap on his father's horse, or after a fall from some old Ontario maple tree. And maybe not. The nameless soldier might have been wounded more recently—in a drunken brawl in a Montréal alleyway or maybe in a fistfight over a gambling debt outside some Toronto flophouse. The young man may have joined General Middleton's militia to get away from the law back East.

Not that it mattered to Gabriel. War does not require a man to know the life of his enemy. And as the company of Canadian soldiers made its final rush on what was left of the defences at Batoche, the Métis general was not pondering the biography of the man in his sights. Dumont squinted slightly and then pulled the trigger, sending the fair-haired soldier tumbling to the ground with a slug to his chest, his blood spilling onto the short grass of the Saskatchewan prairie. Whatever the young man's story was, it came to an abrupt and untimely end early in the afternoon of May 12, 1885, in the last hours of the North-West Rebellion.

Dumont's sharp eye caught another target even before the blond man hit the ground. Cocking the lever of his rifle, Dumont fired again, felling another Canadian soldier just moments after the first. He cocked his Winchester yet again and was about to take another shot when an angry hail of bullets swept over the rifle pit where he was entrenched. The veteran plainsman ducked low as bullets whistled over his head, tore into the log bulwarks in front of him and riddled the ground on either side of his covered position. Dumont risked a glance at the other rifle pits that spread out on either side of him, arrayed in two long lines stretching between the advancing Canadian soldiers and the town of Batoche.

The situation was teetering between desperate and hopeless. Of the roughly 200 Métis who manned the rifle pits three days previously, only about 90 remained. Métis casualties had been remarkably light during the daylight fighting, but each passing night saw numerous desertions from Dumont's forces. A severe shortage of ammunition, coupled with the overwhelming prospect of keeping nearly 900 well-armed Canadians at bay for another day, whittled away the defenders' resolve and their numbers. By the time the Canadians made their final charge on Batoche at around 1 PM on May 12, most of the Métis who still manned their rifle pits were completely out of bullets and had resorted to firing bolts, stones and nails from their rifles.

Dumont knew that these last defenders might easily be overwhelmed by the Canadian rush and called out to a young runner who was cowering in the rifle pit a few yards beside his. He shouted above the roar of cannon and crack of rifle fire.

"Tell Patrice Fleury to cross the river with his men! We can't hold this position for long!"

The boy jumped out of the rifle pit and ran pell-mell through the woods, across Batoche and up to the eastern bank of the South Saskatchewan River, signalling Patrice Fleury and his contingent of 30 fighters to reinforce Dumont's position. The men began ferrying across at once, but they were quickly turned back by a Canadian artillery barrage that would surely have sunk their vessel had they continued. Fleury and his men would not be able to join the fight for Batoche that day.

Meanwhile, pressure was increasing on the Métis front lines as the Canadians continued their advance. Dumont ordered his men to make a fighting retreat to the second line of rifle pits. Gabriel himself withdrew only after every man along the line had pulled back. He turned to the only other fighter in his rifle pit, 93-year-old Joseph Ouellette, who laid down a steady cover fire with Dumont while their fellow Métis retreated.

"Come now, Joseph, we have to fall back," Gabriel barked in French to the venerable old hunter, who had been born in the last century when the *voyageurs* were making their epic portages west, and the enormous buffalo herds still blanketed the Plains.

Ouellette nodded at Dumont, and the countless wrinkles of his ancient face twisted into a look of careless valour. It took Dumont a moment or two before he realised that Ouellette was smiling.

"Lead the way, Gabriel!" the old man hollered over the din of battle.

Dumont swung his rifle over his shoulder and vaulted out of the pit, stopping on the open ground to help his near-skeletal companion up out of the trench. The charging Canadians were almost right on them now, no farther than 60 yards away.

Dumont dropped to one knee and emptied his rifle as Ouellette made for the pit, moving as fast as his emaciated legs could take him.

"Damn all this running about!" Gabriel heard the old man yell. "Just give me a place to sit and shoot."

Smiling in spite of himself, Dumont turned and dashed towards the trench Ouellette had just disappeared into. Gabriel was broad-shouldered and barrel-chested; but he moved with remarkable speed and a surprising, if somewhat brutish, grace. He covered the distance in a few short seconds, bullets whistling overhead and kicking up the earth at his heels. Vaulting into the rifle pit, Dumont found Ouellette loading his rifle through tortured gasps. The Métis general took a quick look through the log bulwarks.

"How're you doing, old man?" Gabriel asked, casting his eyes over the enemy.

The Canadians seemed to be hesitating now, although Dumont couldn't for the life of him understand why. He knew that, with their numbers, all the Canadians had to do was press the attack, and the Métis defences would crumble. His fighters had neither the ammunition nor the manpower to stand against Middleton's soldiers now.

"How do you think I'm doing?" Ouellette shot back, finally catching his breath. "Legs as old as these shouldn't be asked to run." The aged hunter propped his rifle atop the bulwarks and peered out at potential targets. "But my eyes are still good enough to see *les anglais*."

Dumont was just about to ask his companion what he thought the Canadians were waiting for when a deep battle cry sounded from the Canadian camp. A fresh wave of 200 Canadians suddenly crested the hill overlooking Batoche. An officer standing in the centre of the line took off his hat and waved it above his head. The Canadians let out another cheer and charged, their bayonets gleaming in the midday sun.

"Here they come!" shouted Joseph Ouellette, who immediately opened up on the coming soldiers.

The entire Métis line sprang to life, as every man with anything to shoot levelled his rifle at the Canadians and fired. But Dumont knew this fight was nearly over, that his men would not be able to hold against the determined charge. Already, panicked men were abandoning their rifle pits, fleeing before the terrifying sight of the approaching enemy. Gabriel looked back at his beloved Batoche.

"It's over," he whispered to himself.

For a brief moment Gabriel stood absolutely still in his rifle pit, paralysed by that dreadful realization, unable to act as the wall of bayonets drew closer and as more and more of his men fled their posts. In another moment, most of the Métis were in an all-out rout, fleeing in a disorganized mass.

The sound of Ouellette's rifle awakened Dumont to the moment. The fight raged on. He reached back into his ammunition satchel for cartridges. Yet, as the Métis general loaded his Winchester, he found to his surprise that his hands were shaking uncontrollably. Gabriel just stood there, puzzled, not knowing what to make of his trembling appendages.

In all his years on the Plains, throughout all of his adventures, in the face of countless dangers, Dumont had never once lost his nerve. Certainly, he was afraid on more than one occasion, but he had always been in possession of more than enough gumption to see himself through. Yet, here he was now, unable to steady his hands in the moment that Batoche was about to fall. And when it dawned on Dumont that his hands weren't shaking in fear, but in anger, he was able to drive the cartridge into the chamber.

He was angry with himself, at his inability to lead his people to victory. His imminent defeat was no surprise. Over the previous weeks, the Métis general had recognized more than once that things looked bleak, and at some point, while mulling

Gabriel Dumont, taken in the 1880s, holding his gun, which he always called "Le Petit"

over the odds, the tactician in him must have conceded that triumph over the Canadians was impossible. But Gabriel had not given up hope, as irrational as he knew that hope was. Now failure was staring him in the face, and his heart broke.

He poked his head above the bulwarks to take a shot. It was the view over the top of the rifle pit that snapped him back to reality. The sight of the charging Canadians, now almost on them, reminded Gabriel of his duty to his people and instantly calmed his shaking hands. His rifle sounded, and a soldier fell a mere 30 yards away.

"Come on, Father!" he bellowed. "We must pull back!"

The elderly hunter did not look away from his rifle sight. "Just a minute; I want to kill another Englishman."

It seemed like a good idea to Dumont. The Canadians were so close that he could clearly hear individual voices. He knew they would be on them any time now.

"All right then," Gabriel said. "Let us die here."

He was only able to get one shot off before four soldiers dove into the rifle pit. Dumont turned around in time to see one of the men drive his bayonet into Ouellette. Run through the stomach, the ancient hunter died quickly, without a sound. Dumont moved fast. He shot one man point blank and lunged at the other three, brandishing his rifle like a club. Two of the soldiers fell, laid low by the butt of Dumont's rifle; the third man ran out of the pit, terrified at the sight of the enraged Métis. Casting one last look at the body of Joseph Ouellette, Gabriel made the sign of the cross and dashed out of the rifle pit, running towards Batoche, barely one step ahead of the charging Canadians. Batoche was lost, and the Métis were defeated, but Gabriel Dumont was not yet ready to give up. Indeed, as he ran through the streets of Batoche that day, Dumont swore to keep the Métis rebellion alive, even if he was the last man standing against the Canadians.

"à la façon du pays"

Long before any talk of a Métis nation, the Métis people were an established fact in the great northwest of the New World.

Some have quipped that the first Métis was born roughly nine months after the arrival of the first *voyageur* in the West. Human nature being what it is, and the ways of the West being what they were, this statement is probably not far from the truth. *Coureurs de bois* who penetrated into the land beyond the Great Lakes in the 17th century, certainly took Native wives *à la façon du pays*, which is French for "in the fashion of the country." They married according to the customs of the Native tribes with whom they traded and without the services of a priest.

Most of the men who married this way were French, although some Irish, English and Scots traders took Native brides as well. The French, with their hardy *joie de vie* and more adventurous natures, seemed to have made more and better contacts among the Native tribes than their more stodgy British counterparts. Cree brides proved to be the preferred choice among these men. Early travellers through the West noted their beauty, and perhaps more importantly, Cree women seemed apt converts to Christianity and were more inclined to help their husbands in the fur-trade business. Although it is true that many of the relationships were usually temporary and practical, with favoured Native wives often being passed around among the traders, strong and genuine bonds of lasting affection were not unknown.

Gabriel Dumont's roots were found in this frontier practice. His grandfather, Jean-Baptiste Dumont, set out from Montréal in the 1790s to seek his fortune in the burgeoning western fur trade. Moving back and forth between the Saskatchewan valley and Edmonton House, Jean-Baptiste took up with a Sarcee woman known only as Josette "Sarcisse" in 1794. Josette had previously been living with a fur trader by the name of Bruneau and had borne him one child before marrying Gabriel's grandfather. Their union produced two children, Gabriel—the uncle after whom the Gabriel Dumont of legend was named—in 1794, and Jean-Baptiste, Jr., in 1801. Shortly after the birth of their second child, Jean-Baptiste returned to Lower Canada, passing Josette along to another trader named Paul Durant.

About two years later, Jean-Baptiste returned to the West, this time to stay. While no one can say for sure what prompted Jean-Baptiste to abandon eastern society, he wasn't the only man who had difficulty with the adjustment to civilization after a stint in the western hinterlands. Many of the *coureurs de bois* in the 17th and 18th centuries found it difficult to return to the stolid life of farming and "accepting one's place," in the strict and class-bound society of Lower Canada after having had a taste of freedom out west. Unfortunately, on Jean-Baptiste's return, Durant was reluctant to yield up Josette. Dumont evidently felt some strong attachment to his former wife and their children because he took the Sarcee woman back by force. After their reunion, the two had a third child, Isidore, in 1808.

By this time, the first Métis children had already begun to take over the roles of their fathers and grandfathers in the far-flung fur trade of the West. They trapped, hunted and traded while acting as guides, boatmen and labourers for the two great trading companies that dominated the territory at the time— the North West Company (NWC) and the Hudson's Bay Company (HBC). As long as the two corporations remained locked in competition, the Métis had plenty of employment.

But the arrangement did not last. The two companies' rivalry over ever-dwindling fur supplies eventually led into a fierce trading war. A harsh and often violent clash of competing interests, the corporate warfare between the NWC Nor'Westers and the HBC raged throughout the first two decades of the 19th century. The two parties became immersed in a quagmire of lawsuits as battles over the companies' territorial jurisdictions made the vast lands of the North-West into a commercial battlefield. Gangs from opposing companies confronted one another with warrants for each other's arrest, sabotaged trading routes and confiscated goods. On more than one occasion, these confrontations ended in bloodshed and loss of life.

The worst episode of violence occurred in 1816. Thomas Douglas, the Fifth Earl of Selkirk, was a major shareholder in the HBC and was intent on pursuing a scheme to open up the North-West to colonization and agriculture. Acquiring a land grant of 185,000 square miles located around the forks of the Assiniboine and Red Rivers, Selkirk financed the emigration of dispossessed farmers from the United Kingdom. The NWC bitterly opposed Selkirk's plan because his colony interfered with the NWC's supply system to its far-flung traders. In 1814, when the colony's governor, Robert Semple, issued an edict that prohibited the export of any provisions from the region, the Nor'Westers decided to act. Encouraging the Métis to oppose Selkirk's settlers, representatives from the company planted fears (well founded) that the incoming farmers would be a threat to their traditional, nomadic way of life.

Young Métis men, many of whom had come to rely on the buffalo hunt for subsistence, were all too eager to take action. In 1814, Métis hunters with loaded rifles confronted colony administrators to secure the NWC food supplies for the coming season. Throughout 1815, Métis horsemen terrorized the settlers, destroying their crops, torching farmhouses and stealing farmers' horses and their tools. Events culminated a year later, in the spring of 1816, when the inevitable clash between the colony authority and the recalcitrant Métis finally occurred. The Métis eventually came to celebrate the confrontation, enshrining it in their lore as the "Battle of Seven Oaks;" others called it a brutal massacre, and much later, in the interests of political correctness, it was termed the Seven Oaks "Incident."

In a handful of bloody minutes, a contingent of Métis under the command of Cuthbert Grant faced off against Governor Robert Semple and a retinue of assembled colonists. The outcome of the exchange was decidedly in favour of the Métis, who

Cuthbert Grant (1793–1854), leader of the Métis forces at the Battle of Seven Oaks

lost only one man in exchange for 21 Selkirk settlers, including Semple. The famous Métis bard, Pierre Falcon, immortalized Grant's proud victory in song, which became the unofficial anthem of its people, transmitted orally for decades. It was this resistance against Selkirk's colonists that imbued the sons and daughters of the fur trade with common purpose and marked the origin of a Métis sense of nationhood.

In some ways, this development might have been anticipated. The Métis were an in-between people. Not fully accepted by either their Native or European ancestral peoples, some sort of distinct self-concept was bound to develop. We can see it reflected in their language. In English, the Métis were commonly referred to as "Half-breeds" well into the 20th century. The French called them *bois brulé*, for their darker skin that the French likened to the colour of charred wood. Neither label was terribly complimentary, and the people themselves came to prefer the more neutral term Métis, from the French verb *metisser*, meaning, "to mix breeds."

The Métis were just such a mix—a fusion of cultures that soon began to develop along its own path. Language, again, reflects these changes. The Métis became renowned as apt linguists across the North-West. While they retained French for dealing with the traders from the East, their roles as nomadic traders and hunters also required them to learn many of the Native tongues. The language they used among themselves was a mixture of French nouns and Cree verbs. The Cree vocabulary was well suited to words of action. Indeed, some who have studied it call the language one gigantic verb. Certainly, the colourful, expressive Cree actions were better suited to the gregarious Métis, who were often inclined to grandiose expression. For example, in Cree, the word January is literally "the moon of exploding trees," and August "the moon of the flying up of young ducks." Out of this fusion developed a unique language known as *Michif* that the Métis used among themselves.

Things changed dramatically for the Métis in 1821. That was the year the Hudson's Bay Company and Nor'Wester brass decided their war had grown too costly and negotiated a merger. So it was that the bitter rivals were made into a single organization, assuming the title of the original fur monopoly in the North-West: the Hudson's Bay Company. Although the 1821 merger restored a certain stability in the West, it caused no small degree of social upheaval among the Métis. Those Métis who had been previously employed by the Nor'Westers suddenly found themselves out of work, and with the Hudson's Bay consolidating under the stringently parsimonious George Simpson, few new fur-trading opportunities remained. Thus, with more and more Métis no longer directly employed in the fur trade, they turned to the job of feeding it.

After 1821, the Métis took up the lucrative buffalo hunt in increasing numbers. While they made good use of buffalo fur and meat for themselves and anyone interested in purchasing, the most important commodity they produced was pemmican. It was the one provision the Hudson's Bay Company considered a necessity. Pemmican, a Cree word meaning, "manufactured grease," was about appealing to the taste buds as it sounds. This frontier staple was prepared by taking dried buffalo meat and dried berries or fruit and crushing them together into a powder that was then mixed with fat or boiled marrow. Despite this less-than-appetizing process, pemmican served a vital role. With its high calorie content and a shelf life that could be measured in decades, it has been called the "fuel" that powered the North-West fur-trading network, especially in the more northerly, less hospitable trading posts.

Some of the Métis turned to small scale-farming after the Nor'Westers merged with the HBC. Most supplemented their incomes by continuing, at least to some degree, in their hereditary roles as guides, boatmen, trappers and traders. Still, the great summer buffalo hunts became a central fixture in Métis culture for two generations, ensuring that the Métis continued to live at least a semi-nomadic life.

Such was the state of affairs in the North-West when the Dumont clan grew to frontier prominence. Throughout his life, the family patriarch Jean-Baptiste worked as a freeman on contract for numerous HBC posts in the North Saskatchewan valley. But on the heels of the merger of 1821, each of his three sons—Gabriel, Jean-Baptiste, Jr., and Isidore—pursued the buffalo and the life that went with it.

All of Jean-Baptiste's sons were imposing men. Each standing over 6 feet tall, they were huge specimens for that era. Gabriel, however, seems to have been the largest both in stature and presence. He was, apparently, a notorious firebrand in his younger days. One story tells of a gambling spree that lasted for three days and nights without pause and with no more sustenance than a steady downing of whiskey. In another tale, after a heroic bout with rum, Dumont killed a man in some sort of gambling altercation. When the victim's stepfather pursued Gabriel looking for retribution, Dumont beat him and left him for dead. Still, the apparently vicious Gabriel, Sr., did settle down in his later years, eventually becoming the recognized leader of a sizeable Métis community at Lac Ste. Anne.

Jean-Baptiste's youngest son Isidore wed a Métis woman named Louise Laframboise in 1833. The two settled in the Red River district for a time. The Red River area was the main centre of Métis life in the West during this period. When they were not on the buffalo hunt, larger and larger numbers of Métis congregated there. An area of land that lay along the drainage of three large North American rivers—the Missouri, the Mississippi and the Red—which emptied into what is now known as Lake Winnipeg, the Red River region was a perfectly situated trading centre. Trade, led to settlement, which in turn attracted agriculture and the fervent missionaries who spread the Catholic faith. Life on the Red River was far more settled than the traditional Métis way, but the great annual summer buffalo hunts were still the dominant feature of Métis culture. Such was the life that Isidore and Louise were living in 1837 when their third child, Gabriel, named after his uncle, was born.

Le Petit

Gabriel grew up in the West when the buffalo were still plentiful. His home was a typical frontier abode: a log cabin held together by a system of mortised and tenoned dovetail joints, a story and a half high with a roof of sod and hay. The windows were sheets of rawhide scraped thin and stretched across openings in the walls, only allowing a faint light into the rustic room. Bricks were not readily available, so many of the Métis made their chimneys out of wooden poles covered in a thick layer of clay plaster. Inside, the fireplace was a crucial source of heat during the harsh prairie winters.

As for the furnishings, most of the Métis of this period made their own furniture. Built in a simple, dependable style, the furnishings and accommodation in Métis homes were sparse. The first and often the only room of the house usually held little more in the way of furniture than a table and a few chairs. Most homes had one bed, which was reserved for the parents, leaving the children to sleep atop buffalo-robe mattresses that were laid out on the floor.

Young Gabriel's diet would have consisted primarily of whatever his father culled from the prairie. It would have been a meat-heavy menu—buffalo meat, cooked, smoked or dried was available in great volume, along with the occasional smoked fish and venison. *Tourtieres*, pastry crusts stuffed with meat and baked, were often filled with the delicate meat of the passenger pigeons that flocked to the thickets and woods. The women also made cakes, pies and jams from the wild berries that grew in the area. And, of course, there was the ever-present pemmican, which a Métis child couldn't get away from, as hard as he or she may have tried.

Life in the home, of course, was more than simply food and shelter. While the lives of these gregarious Métis were by no means centred within the confines of their humble cabins, more than a few traditions were borne out under their sod roofs. The home was largely the mother's domain, where she and her children stayed during the day. She cooked, managed the house, served as a schoolteacher to the children and made sure they learned their prayers. It was in their homes that Métis mothers led their children through their nightly prayers, some of the more devout reciting the entire rosary before wrapping themselves up in their buffalo-robe blankets.

The Métis men did their part to educate their children as well, passing on an entirely different sort of knowledge to the boys who would one day take their place on the hunting grounds. At night, the men gathered around fires, waxing nostalgic about past hunting trips, entertaining one another with stories of adventures and regaling the children with tall tales and folklore. Much of the Métis culture was passed on during these story-telling sessions. Native legends rubbed shoulders with Christian parables, along with the ghost stories and superstitions their French fathers brought from Lower Canada. Wide-eyed children sat transfixed as their elders spoke of ghosts, werewolves and flying canoes.

Along with the rest of his peers, Gabriel Dumont would have acquired much of his early understanding of the world during these evenings. Yet this was only one phase of a Métis boy's education. As the youngsters grew, they began the process of earning their place in the rough and tumble world of the prairies. Children were encouraged to watch their parents carefully, learning proper conduct and the laws of survival that dictated so much of the Métis activities. As young girls learned how to skin buffalo and prepare pemmican, boys absorbed the rules of the hunt and acquired a near-obsessive preoccupation with marksmanship. They began practising with makeshift bows and arrows, shooting at anything they could call a target—prairie dogs, birds, berries, hares and whatever else the prairie could supply. These youngsters held regular competitions with one another and awarded the best shot with some token prize—a brass button, a quiver of arrows, a ripe fruit. The ongoing contests inadvertently made them into apprentice hunters, honing their skills for the day they would ride to the hunt with their fathers.

Even early on in his life, during these youthful testing grounds for the hunt, Gabriel Dumont could not help but distinguish himself from the other boys. A fearless child, Gabriel was imbued with a fiercely competitive nature, always eager to test his measure in any kind of contest. During his boyhood years, he established himself something of as a frontier wunderkind. He was a skilled equestrian by age 10, breaking horses alongside Métis men. Fleet of foot, young Gabriel regularly set crowds of children cheering when he went after rabbits; it was said he could chase any hare on foot until the creature dropped from exhaustion. He was a natural boatman, able to handle a canoe over turbulent waters, and was blessed with an inexplicable talent at fishing, always bringing home enough catch to provide a modest feast. Rare for the Métis, Gabriel was also a capable and powerful swimmer from an early age.

But of all these skills, the most important was marksmanship. Just as the best riflemen were amongst the most respected men in Métis society, the children who were proficient with bow and arrow were lauded over their peers. It wasn't long after Gabriel fashioned his first bow that he proved to be matchless with the old Native weapon. Training himself to be a crack shot, young Dumont sought out older Native boys from the tribes his family came into contact with, challenging them to archery competitions—challenges which he regularly won. Such bold behaviour caught the eye of the older Métis, who laughed and nodded appreciatively at the skill and bravery of this budding hunter.

As popular as Gabriel Dumont had become amongst his peers and his elders, he was still denied the use of a gun, deemed too young to take this first symbolic step to manhood. That would come in his 11th year.

It was the summer of 1848, and Gabriel's father decided to leave Fort Pitt on the North Saskatchewan, which had served as his family's home base over the last several years, and head back east to the Red River country. A few other families under Isidore's leadership made the trek as well. They packed their families and possessions onto their the Red River carts and began the journey eastward, fording the imposing Saskatchewan River before turning southwards towards Fort Ellice near the Qu'Appelle River.

Here, the small Métis caravan crossed a hunting area traditionally disputed by the Cree and the aloof, warlike Sioux. Relations between the Métis and the Natives were often shaky; even those Native tribes with whom the Métis were friendly would often react unpredictably when encountered on the prairie. Violence could erupt between a group of Métis hunters and Natives from a tribe thought to be amiable. As for the Sioux, any Métis running into braves from that militant tribe would expect violence.

Isidore and the two other patriarchs in the small caravan were well aware that they might be in danger as they made their way south, and the customary good humour and gaiety of the journey was replaced by a tense alertness. One evening, after the men had pulled their carts into a defensive circle around the campsite, young Gabriel was sent to start a smudge fire upwind of the camp to keep the ravenous prairie mosquitoes at bay.

He and his younger brother Isidore were gathering brush in a small wood atop a hillock not far from the camp, when Gabriel heard the distant, rumbling sound of hooves galloping across the plains. The boy's imagination came to life as in his mind's eye he envisioned a mighty Sioux war party thundering across the prairie towards the small caravan. In less time than it takes to swat a mosquito, Gabriel dropped his bundle of wood, grabbed young Isidore by the arm and rushed back to the camp.

"Father! Father!" Gabriel cried. "There are horsemen coming!"

The camp instantly sprung to life. Men cursed as they went for their hunting rifles, while the women quickly stamped out the campfires. Gabriel ran to his father as the Métis hunter was barking orders.

"I am not afraid, father!" he shouted, interrupting the veteran Métis hunter. "Give me a gun and let me stand with you."

Isidore stopped for only a moment. "Do not bother me now, Gabriel. You are too young for this. Go to your mother; she will tell you what to do."

Gabriel sulked off, and his father darted away from the ring of Red River carts with another hunter, Petit Cayen, at his side, moving towards the hillock where Gabriel had been collecting wood. As Isidore neared the rise, he could feel and hear the rumbling. He fell to one knee, putting his ear to the ground. The veteran hunter, knowing the sound well, leapt to his feet, a relieved smile stretched across his face.

"Those are no horsemen!" he exclaimed to Cayen. "Those are buffalo!"

Normally, a herd of stampeding buffalo might be just as dangerous as a party of Sioux braves on the warpath, but Isidore knew that this herd would pass his camp without doing any harm. The stampede was approaching from the direction of the wooded rise and would split in two as it approached the natural divide. The Métis had made camp just behind the hill, and they were able to watch from within their protective ring of carts as the buffalo stormed by on either side of them.

After the stampede passed by, the Métis children began teasing young Gabriel for his error, mimicking his panicked warning and laughing about the possibility of Sioux mounted on buffalo. The mocking continued until Gabriel's uncle, Alexis Fisher, silenced the boys.

"Yes, of course, it's easy to laugh now," the Métis hunter said. "But how many of you were jesting just moments ago when you were convinced that the Sioux were coming?" Gabriel's peers looked sheepish in the sudden silence of the prairie night. "If I remember correctly, Gabriel asked for a gun and wanted to fight, while the rest of you ran for the safety of your mother's skirts. He is the only real hunter among you."

Gabriel was only 11 years old, yet he was more than ready to be ranked among the hunters of his people. He flushed with pride when his uncle turned to him. "Well Gabriel, you asked for a gun, and as far as I'm concerned, you deserve one."

With these words, Alexis pulled an old trading musket from one of his carts and presented it to a wide-eyed Gabriel.

"This is yours," Alexis said, smiling proudly as he placed the gun in Gabriel's eager hands. "Tonight, you have proven yourself a man."

It was an impromptu ceremony, carried out under the brilliant starlit canopy of the prairie night, but to Alexis Fisher's credit, Gabriel Dumont would never forget it. Admiration and envy immediately replaced the taunts of his fellow youngsters. Dumont treasured the gun, christening it *Le Petit*, or "The Little One." This was the musket that set him on the road to becoming the most legendary marksman among the Métis. And although Gabriel would own many different rifles throughout the course of his life, he would always call them *Le Petit*, in honour of his uncle and the night he earned his first.

The rest of the journey to the Fort Garry area occurred without further incident. It was already the second major move of Gabriel's young life, but the difficulty of the move was eased by the hospitable welcome the caravan received from the Métis around the fort. Almost immediately upon their arrival, the local Métis called a *corvée*—one of the finest examples of the humanity that existed on the Canadian frontier. It was the Métis version of a barn raising, bringing men and women

from all around to aid in the construction of a home for whatever family was in need of one. Each family was well aware that
they might be the ones moving next season, so the work was
always done in good cheer, quickly and efficiently, with little or
no complaint. No one needed to be asked to participate; for
while the Métis prided themselves on their individual strength
and resourcefulness, they also acknowledged the need for
cooperation, and the strength of a united community. The
corvée was one of the best examples of such an understanding,
and thanks to it, within a matter of days, everyone in Isidore
Dumont's caravan had a place they could call home.

CHAPTER TWO

The Métis Way of Life

To the old-timers in the hunt, the sound of the
Red River carts in motion sounded like home.

NEITHER THE MÉTIS NOR ONE of their most famous sons, Gabriel Dumont, can be understood without exploring those grand cavalcades that were the buffalo hunts. These hunts were staple events in the Métis way of life, especially during the first half of Dumont's life. From his earliest days, he was raised, not just in the cabins where his family wintered, but also from the caravans of covered Red River carts as they creaked and groaned their way across the prairie in pursuit of the great buffalo herds. The experiences of the hunt—the unforgettable cacophony of the Red River carts, the smell of gun powder mingled with dust of thousands of buffalo stampeding and the sight of men and women labouring hard to scrape clean the still-bloody buffalo skins—were indelibly imprinted upon him from his first years of life.

Buffalo hunts could occur at any time of year and be of almost any scale. A lone Métis hunter with a hungry family might trudge out into the deep snow of late winter, approaching a herd of buffalo downwind, until he was close enough to fire from what the Métis called "blasting range." He perhaps offered a prayer to the Virgin Mary that his aim would be true. A wounded, enraged bull buffalo was no treat to deal with even from the relative safety of a fleet and well-trained horse, let alone on foot and mired in the deep snow.

More commonly, however, the Métis went on group hunts any time from late spring to early autumn. Some Métis would even go on multiple hunts in the same year—spring, summer and fall. Smaller groups of a few closely related hunters were far from unknown, but the advantages of scale tended to encourage larger groups. A large hunt was better able to defend itself against a Native attack, and it was also better able to collectively process slaughtered buffalo. Last, but certainly not least, to such a convivial people as the Métis, the hunts had an important social component. Large-scale hunts that involved hundreds of participants gathering and setting forth from larger settlements on the prairie became a seasonal tradition.

The choice to mount an expedition would have been made by a group of leading Métis, who would send out the word as quickly as possible. News of an impending hunt spread quickly throughout the community from parish to parish, greeted with enthusiasm by those eager to shake the dust of previous months' sedentary living from their feet. All hunters intending to join the hunt were called to meet at a central place to discuss a time for departure, decide on a leader and appoint his council of captains.

The leader and the council operated as a moving government while the Métis caravan was camped on the open prairie. These were important men, whose word was law for the duration of the hunt, so they were always chosen with care and sobriety in semi-religious ceremonies that were presided over by a local missionary. The appointed men were usually the most respected members of their community. Gabriel's father, Isidore, often led hunts or served as one of the captains. Gabriel himself would have the most impressive track record on the hunt, being called on to lead practically every hunt he had participated in from the remarkably young age of 25 until the last of the buffalo hunts in the 1870s.

The Rules of the Hunt were well established and fixed by tradition, but they were set out and explicitly agreed upon beforehand by all participants regardless, so that no man might say he was unaware of the crimes and their consequences. The following are the rules as recorded by Alexander Ross in 1840:

The Rules of the Hunt
1. *No buffalo to be run on Sabbath day.*
2. *No party to fork off, lag behind, or go before without permission.*
3. *No person or party to run buffalo before the general order.*
4. *Every captain with his men, in turn, to patrol the camp and keep guard.*
5. *For the first trespass against these laws, the offender to have his saddle and bridle cut up.*
6. *For the second offence, the coat to be taken off the offender's back and be cut up.*
7. *For the third offence, the offender to be flogged.*
8. *Any person convicted of theft, even to the value of a sinew, to be brought to the middle of the camp, the crier to call out his or her name three times, adding the word "Thief" at each time.*

While the Métis were generally a community-minded people, their young men were also known for their recklessness and bravado. Youthful hunters sometimes got caught up in the excitement of the hunt, rushing herds prematurely and getting close to animals that other men may have been aiming for. The rules were meant to restrain such behaviour, even though the penalties imposed for breaking the rules were generally quite minor, rarely resulting in any kind of corporal punishment. Rather, they struck at an offender's standing in the community and depended upon the loss of face and honour to act as a deterrent.

Still, the rules were not always obeyed, nor were the specified punishments always imposed. The leader of the hunt could bend them any way he saw fit. Gabriel, for example, is said to have once harshly judged a Métis and a Native who had gone ahead of a hunt that he led, giving the two a sound thrashing when neither man had ever broken a rule of the hunt before. Then again, on another occasion, he was more merciful than the rules dictated with two youths who had erred for the third time by interfering with a buffalo herd by riding ahead prematurely. Instead of the flogging that the infringement called for, he lay a fierce tongue-lashing on the pair. Then again, the two might not have felt so fortunate at the time, for Gabriel's tirade was cruel enough to have earned transmission throughout a century of Métis tales.

The leaders chosen and the rules agreed to, the often-huge hunting caravans would lumber out onto the ocean of grama grass that was the great prairie. For the Métis who had grown up with this seasonal exodus, the beginning of the hunt was a magical time, where the air was buzzed with excitement and the expectation of adventure. Years of seasonal travel instilled an almost inborn travel lust in every Métis man, woman and child, so that the departure for the hunting grounds was always a cause for celebration.

They were often enormous caravans. Alexander Ross, first historian of the Red River district, accompanied the buffalo hunt in June 1840 where he counted 1210 Red River carts,

620 hunters, 650 women, 360 children, 1058 horses, 568 oxen and 542 dogs. Arranged into three parallel lines of shouting children, scolding mothers, eager hunters, neighing horses and yipping dogs, the hunting train must have been a quite sight to see.

Without fail, every first-time observer could not help but notice the tremendous din that invariably rose from these massive processions. The huge, recently formed packs of dogs that ran yipping, growling and barking alongside were but an accompaniment to the main "music" of the carts themselves. The Red River carts became such a part of Métis life that the Cree developed a hand signal—two forefingers curled around, forming a shape of wagon wheels—to represent their strange Métis cousins, the "wagon men."

The Red River carts were the product of the hybrid culture of the Métis. The design was based on the simple cart that was used by the ancestors of the Métis forefathers in the villages of Medieval Europe. But over time, the Métis applied their ingenuity and peerless knowledge of the Plains and its available supplies to modify and improve the basic design. For example, the carts were made entirely out of wood with only a few strips of tough buffalo hide used as fasteners. The use of readily available materials meant that repairs could always be made whenever a breakdown occurred on the plains, the supply of wood and leather always being plentiful. Moreover, avoiding the use of metal made for a lighter cart, so if the cart was bogged down in mud or muskeg, it was easier to rescue. When the Métis had to cross waterways on their journeys, the wheels could be removed and fastened under the cart. The whole cart-cum-barge then simply floated across the water.

But the sound of the wheel hubs grinding away at the axle, wood on naked wood, was a sound never to be forgotten, however hard the listener might try. Nor could the axles be greased because the dust of the plains would rise at the cart's passage and stick to the grease, quickly forming a thick

If ever there was an example of a technology perfectly suited to the needs of those who used it, certainly it was the Métis' Red River cart. It is unclear when the cart first came into use, but it was certainly popular by the early 1800s. The cart was made entirely of wood, held together with leather straps, and pulled by a horse or an ox strapped to two poles extended from the axle. Over the years, the Red River cart was subject to various modifications, but these basic characteristics remained unchanged. The carts were originally rather small, with three-foot solid wheels cut from large trees, and capable of transporting up to 450 pounds. Later, larger wheels with four spokes came into use, and eventually huge, many-spoked wheels appeared, enabling the cart to carry nearly twice as much as it had originally. The large wheels removed most of the challenge of travelling through thick, sticky mud or over hard, baked prairie, and they could easily be removed to allow the cart to float across rivers. Alas, no technology is perfect, and the flaw in the Red River cart was the shrieking of the wheels as they ground against the axles. The wheels could not be greased since lubricants mixed with the dust and dirt thrown up from the trail caused damage to the axle. There was no respite from the ear-jarring noise, which could be heard for long distances.

cement around the moving parts. Newcomers to the area described the sound as "hellish," "horrifying" or "nerve-wracking." Imagine an entire classroom of children's nails scraping on a chalkboard—that would be the sound of but one cart. The expeditions often contained hundreds, and so the Métis announced their presence to all God's creatures for miles around. To the old-timers in the hunt, the sound of the Red River carts in motion sounded like home.

A strict military discipline was maintained in certain aspects of the hunt. As the sun began its march across the sky each morning, the chosen guide for that day's travel raised a large white flag above the camp for all to see. This signal let everyone know that they had a half-hour to prepare to move out. The columns then set off behind the guide in a pre-determined, strictly kept order. The wagon columns were arranged so that they might be pulled into a defensive *ronde* as quickly as possible in the face of impending attack. Any change to the travelling order would thus disturb the carefully made plans to circle the wagons and potentially risk the safety of the entire hunt.

At night and during the day, pairs of scouts dispersed in all directions around the main body, acting as the eyes and ears of the hunt, and ensuring its safety. Good scouting was crucial, especially when the caravans passed through Sioux lands. It was customary to pair a younger, inexperienced man with a veteran hunter in these reconnaissance teams, ensuring that knowledge would be passed from generation to generation. The common practice was to leave one man in hiding, and he would observe the other's advance to investigate potentially hostile territory. Thus, the man in hiding always had a chance to either support his comrade with the advantage of surprise, or gallop back to warn his fellows if the danger proved too great.

The education of the younger men was not always such serious business, however. As the caravan screeched and rumbled over the tall grass of the plains, the men were happy to test each other's skills at any opportunity. A hare spotted on the prairies would elicit a wild chase, where mounted hunters spurred their horses and set out after their quarry, riding at full tilt, coming within a hair's breadth of one another as each man vied to bring down the unfortunate prey. Intensely competitive, the hunters didn't give an inch during these chases, galloping neck-and-neck, cutting each other off, shoving riders out of their way, risking life and limb in their pursuit. If such activity was thought foolhardy, the Métis owed much of their unparalleled horsemanship to these competitions.

Of course, such proud displays of warrior skill were not purely for the benefit of their fellow riders. Single Métis hunters were always conscious that they were performing before scores of unwed young women. Many marriages found their beginnings in these hunting excursions. While the men tried their best to look indifferent, their ready and abundant displays of frontier machismo were more for the benefit of the women than anyone else.

A hunt was serious business, but the Métis still made room for joy and socializing; it was their nature. Especially during the midsummer, the Métis would divide the day into two equal travelling periods, which were separated by a midday prairie siesta. A full lunch, which included a cooked meal and copious rounds of the hot, dark tea that the Métis were famous for, was followed by an afternoon nap. In the evening, after the caravan pulled into a defensive circle, the livestock cared for and the general hustle and bustle of setting camp subsided, the social aspects of the hunt heated up again.

The family tents ("lodges") were set up, and the women gathered in small groups to prepare supper and chatter away. Children were responsible for combing the surrounding prairie for fuel, and they brought back willow, sun-bleached aspen and dried buffalo dung for the cooking fires. The food consisted mostly of whatever small game the land provided.

Ducks, snipe, prairie chicken and grouse were common fare. When the meals were prepared, the Métis women called their families together, and they enjoyed their meals on the grass, protected from the infamous swarms of prairie mosquitoes by the smudge fires the children lit around the camp.

Every night, a short time after supper, the leader of the hunt made his rounds through camp, calling his people to prayer. The missionaries would have prepared a travelling altar inside an open tent—likely a rough-hewn little table covered with a white cloth and bedecked with flowers in honour of the Virgin Mary. The call to worship brought every hunter and his family around the makeshift church within minutes. And so began the service, with the presiding Catholic missionary leading the congregation in prayer. They prayed for their safety, for a bountiful hunt and for the blessing of their priest and the holy sacraments. As sombre as they were, evening Masses seldom lasted long, and after they were over, the worshippers dispersed into the night.

Religious obligations fulfilled, the Métis regrouped around night fires that were stirred back to life. There they passed the rest of the evening in celebration—drinking, singing and carrying on in fine Métis fashion. Songs, legends, war stories and exaggerated memories were freely exchanged. It was around these fires that young men and women made their first awkward courting attempts and old friends and relatives who had been apart for months or years caught up with news. The happy chatter merged with the usual chorus of the prairie night—the howling call of wolves, the yipping of the prairie dogs and coyotes and the distant, defiant bellowing of bull buffalo.

"The signal is given!"

Such was life in the buffalo hunt, but as joyous as it could be, socializing was not its purpose. Many families were dangerously short on food after the long winter months, and when the columns of carts finally drew close enough to a large herd, the anticipation of the impending hunt superseded everything else. The men selected their swiftest chargers, double-checked their muskets and ammunition and gathered together to advance upon the nearby herd.

"I joined the hunters who were giving vent to their exuberance in a very noisy manner," wrote Father Belcourt, a frontier priest who accompanied a Métis buffalo expedition in 1845. Belcourt remembered riding with the hunters as they came closer to the animals. "We approached at a brisk trot while they continued to graze peaceably. Then we pulled our horses to a walking pace, for they do not stampede until the very last minute when approached quietly." It was the crucial time of the hunt, for the goal was to get as close as possible to the herd without causing a stampede before the hunt leader, his judgement honed by experience, gave the signal to charge. An organized approach ensured the best hunting for all participants; a premature charge on the buffalo sent the animals scattering too early. None but the most foolish would think about shooting until the order was given by the hunt leader.

Father Belcourt remembered that the hunters seemed to be pushing their luck as they slowly approached the herd. "The bulls were apparently not very pleased to see us," Belcourt recalled. "They showed some signs of ill humour. Some stamped their hooves, tossing up clouds of dust. Others rolled on the ground like horses, jumping to their feet again with all the agility of a hare. A few, apparently more conscious of their dignity, watched us fixedly and let escape, from time to time, sharp, hollow bellows. The sharp, jerky twitching of their tails left no doubt that they found our presence just as disagreeable as did their fellows."

This hunt leader's judgement proved sound. Raising one hand high over his head, he let it hang for several seconds

Métis hunters rode specially trained horses called buffalo runners and they followed the chief hunter as close to the herd as possible without being detected. They then fanned out to the right and left. Within 300 yards the buffalo usually became aware of the hunters' presence and began to move. The chief called "trot," and the men began a slow gallop. When the chief called "equa," they attacked the herd, and the "running of the buffalo" was in full force. For an uninitiated bystander, this process would certainly appear chaotic. Stampeding buffalo and swiftly moving horses, cloaked in clouds of dust, danced with a background cacophony of thundering hoofs, bellowing buffalo, shouting Métis and cracking gunfire.

before bringing it down in one curt motion, signalling for the killing to begin. Belcourt remembered the exciting moment: "The signal is given! We whip up our chargers, and the dense, heavy mass before us breaks and flees with surprising speed and lightness." The ranks of hunters descend on the buffalo with all the determination of a cavalry charge, sending their quarry scattering away in every direction.

Belcourt, astride his horse, rode along with the hunters. "Several buffalo are bowled over by the first shots," he wrote of the first few seconds. "Others, mortally wounded and furious, stand at bay, tearing up the ground with their horns or stamping their hooves like rams. From beneath their tight, tangled poll locks, their eyes sparkle with rage, bidding the most intrepid of hunters to keep his distance." After the signal, all is a chaotic, hurtling mass of beasts and men in a swirling miasma of dust and gunpowder. Whereas the Métis approached the buffalo as a unified body, the moment the shooting starts, it is every man for himself.

This method of hunting could be dangerous business. An angry bull buffalo was a fearsome creature, weighing 1800–2000 pounds, measuring 10–12 feet in length and standing 6 feet at the shoulder. Belcourt witnessed the power of one bull that broke out of the slaughter and charged through a line of Métis carts arrayed near the killing ground. The panicked beast caught one of the carts with its horns and sent it flying. The upended cart rolled across the prairie until it settled, axle up, like a discarded toy. Belcourt was stunned by the animal's strength. "These carts, hauled by a horse, usually carry a load of more than 1000 pounds," the priest wrote.

With a flick of its massive head or a sudden lunge, a buffalo could quickly turn the tables on an erstwhile hunter, sending him tumbling to the earth at breakneck speed or into the path of other charging hooves. Worse, the enraged bull might turn on the now hopelessly isolated, immobile man. It was not uncommon for a buffalo hunter to meet his end on the horns of a raging bull—the hunter turned into the hunted in the blink of an eye.

Their blood hot with the danger of the chase and the thrill of the hunt, the Métis whooped as they plunged their chargers into the phalanx of stampeding beasts and discharged their weapons at truly astounding rates. Of course, only the first shot could be loaded and primed before the actual charge. The men carried more balls in their mouths so that they could prime their guns, pour in a charge of powder and then spit shot into the barrel, their saliva causing the shot to stick to the powder at the bottom.

Bullets flew in all directions as the orchestration of the first charge quickly degenerated into chaos. The men struggled to reload and fire quickly while their horses galloped through the fray. It was not uncommon for a man to be accidentally struck by a stray ball. Many of the hunters used muskets that had a dangerous tendency to misfire, and more than one rider was wounded by his own gun. Hunting leaders were often called on to act as field surgeons when riders were wounded.

A leader's approach to such injuries was typically efficient and brutally swift. One such incident occurred in a spring sometime in the 1870s, during a hunt led by Gabriel Dumont. A Cree hunter's musket misfired, reducing the fingers on one hand to a mess of flesh, blood and bone. When Dumont heard of the accident, he promptly quit the hunting ground and rode to where the wounded man was standing, holding the wrist of the wounded hand and trying hard to contain his tears of pain. Dumont took one quick look at the badly mangled fingers before giving the Native man the bad news. He spoke in Cree.

"They have to come off."

The Cree blinked but didn't flinch. "All right. Take them off."

Dumont did not waste time. Using the stock of his rifle as an impromptu operating table, Gabriel spread the man's injured fingers across the gun stock, pulled his heavy hunting knife from his belt and made a few swift strokes. The Cree hunter made no sound throughout the procedure, expecting no sympathy from his brusque surgeon. Once the fingers were gone, Gabriel bound the hand with a piece of sinew that he tied tightly around the wrist.

The Cree, eager to exhibit his toughness, smiled at Dumont and said, "My fingers are not enough to feed your family. You should get back to the buffalo before they get away."

Dumont laughed and patted the man on the back before he leapt on his horse and galloped back to the hunting ground.

Through it all, the hunters depended heavily on the training and innate intelligence of their impressive steeds. Practically flying over the prairie as it overtook its immense yet fleet prey while avoiding the badger and gopher holes in its path, a horse needed to be perfectly attuned to its rider's wishes, which were often transmitted only by heels and knees as the hunter's hands poured more gunpowder into his muskets. The hunter depended on his mount for his livelihood and for his very life, so it is little wonder that the Métis so highly prized their horses.

"…anything tastes good if you're hungry enough"

The wild charge of the Métis hunters often petered out miles from where it began. Scattered for miles around, the hunters would at last rein in their snorting, gleaming steeds and comb over the ground they had covered. Some hunters would drop gloves or strips of cloth next to the beasts they killed to identify them. Others, more sure of themselves, simply remembered distinguishing features of the buffalo they felled. The best of the hunters could kill between 8 and 12 buffalo in a run.

When he reached his late teens, Dumont was already well on his way to being one of the best buffalo runners the Métis had ever produced. He was an astonishingly good marksman, able to pot a duck through the head at 100 paces. Acquiring his skill on horseback in his earliest years, he became more proficient as he grew from a rangy youth into a sinewy young man. In short, Gabriel Dumont came to embody that near-perfect combination of bravery, knowledge of country and animal, horsemanship, timing, judgement and marksman-ship characteristic of the legendary Plains buffalo hunters. Legend has it that he reached such a level of skill as a hunter that he did not even have to go to the buffalo, but rather, was able to convince the buffalo to come to him. For it is said that somewhere along the way, Dumont picked up that rare art—almost unheard of among the Métis and dying off among the Natives—of calling the buffalo. A hunter could lie in wait in the woods, making the sound of a buffalo, and the beasts would come to him.

With his prodigious skills, Gabriel was more than able to provide for his family while emerging as a leader among his people. Métis custom held that the best buffalo runners ded-icate the kills from at least one run through the herd to those in the community who could not provide for themselves—the old, the infirm or those too poor to own a horse. Dumont always had a soft place in his heart for the less fortunate and never failed to provide generously for them.

After the shooting subsided, the hunters retraced the path they took through the buffalo herd, preparing their kills for butchering. The common practice was to prop the dead animals up on their knees and spread the hind legs out so that most of the buffalo's weight was on its belly. Skinning and butchering quickly followed. The whole camp—men, women and children—threw themselves into the effort to harvest the hard-won skins and meat. It was a communal activity, where one family was happy to help its neighbours, just as these neighbours, in turn, might be happy to give the first some spare pemmican in the hard months of winter.

As the women drove the carts up to the still-warm carcasses, the men unsheathed their hefty hunting knives and cut long slits all the way down the backs of the buffalo. They then removed the hide completely and began butchering. They removed the choice cuts first, cutting out the tongue, the hump and the esophagus. A plentiful hunt might even prompt waste-fulness, where these delicacies might be the only parts har-vested. Indeed, even in the leanest of times, the Métis were hardly known for the economy of their harvesting methods, and they always left behind significant waste for the wolves.

While the men stripped the hair, fat and other impurities from the hides, the women carved up the carcasses, cutting the meat into thin strips. These strips were then laid on grills made of branches, which were placed over smoking buffalo-chip fires. The best quality meat was used by the Métis to make a delicious, chewy jerky that they often carried with them and chewed on like candy.

The lower quality meat was used in the making of that pillar of the fur trade—pemmican. The meat was dried and pounded into powder with a hammer, a bar, a stick or a stone and then put into big cast iron pots full of boiling fat or buffalo marrow. This mixture of pulverised dry meat and fat or marrow was allowed to cook until it congealed into a bubbling paste. Wild berries picked from the plains—saskatoons, wild grapes and chokecherries—were often dried and added to the mix. Such additions were not mandatory, but most seemed to think that the berries improved the taste, at least somewhat.

The boiling hot paste was then poured into bags called parfleches, which were made from buffalo hide and sewn up with tendon or rawhide to form an airtight seal. The bags were left to dry as hard as tallow, either in the sun or hanging from the Red River carts on the return to their wintering homes. Some of the more ambitious cooks allowed the pemmican to age for years, the idea being that the longer pemmican aged, the better it was. Each parfleche intended for sale to the Hudson's Bay Company was supposed to weigh exactly 100 pounds, and so this weight quickly became the adopted standard across the Plains.

Much of the pemmican was sold to fur traders, but the Métis kept and ate some too, especially during the winter months. Hardly a delicacy, pemmican was eaten in a variety of ways. It could be eaten straight out of the bag without any preparation. Some Métis took the time to heat it up, cooking it in its own grease. Many made dumplings from pemmican, folding the buffalo product into dough and boiling it into a stew called *rababout*. In the winter, pemmican would have to be heated before it was eaten because it would freeze to such a hardness that portions had to be cut off with a sturdy axe.

And the taste? Those who tried it for the first time often compared the taste to suet—the hard white fat on the kidneys or loins of animals that was used to make dough. But anyone who subsisted on the fatty frontier provision long enough learned to take something of a liking to it. Perhaps the populace existing on the rough fringes associated the peculiar taste of pemmican with a full stomach—a state of being that was often considered a luxury west of the 100th meridian. Or, as Louis Goulet, a Métis man who may have eaten too much pemmican in his lifetime, put it: "Anything tastes good if you're hungry enough."

The Métis hunting day concluded with the setting sun, but if the herds were still nearby and plentiful, the butchering might continue for days. And the end results could be quite profitable. When the hunting expedition that Father Belcourt

accompanied in 1845 ended on October 16, the priest calculated that the 55 hunters who participated killed about 1776
buffalo. Belcourt calculated that the total worth of the game
equalled roughly £1700 sterling, and after the expenses of the
expedition, left roughly £1500 earned among all the hunters
in fewer than two months, a considerable sum in the mid-
19th century on the Plains or anywhere. Their families thus
provided for, the Métis would then return to the relative safety
of their settlements.

After moving to Red River, Isidore Dumont and his family
participated in these huge hunts. At first the young Gabriel was
not permitted to take part in the running of the buffalo—a
dangerous and testing task even for fully grown men—but in
other ways he had already assumed an adult's role. He shot
small game with his newly won musket, *Le Petit*, helped his
parents as they skinned and butchered buffalo, helped to
swim horses and ferry carts across rivers and assisted in the
making of pemmican.

We lived in peace, but always armed to the teeth.

Along the way, hunters and their families had to be prepared
for many difficulties and dangers. Prairie fires, for example, were
a feared phenomenon in the old North-West. Usually set by
lightning strikes, these fires spread across the tinderbox of dry,
midsummer grassland with frightening speed, destroying
everything in their path. One Métis tactic for coping with the
fires was to "back light" a section of the intervening plains.
These controlled burnings consumed the grassy fuel in the
path of the fire, thus keeping it at bay.

In the calm that prefaced a prairie thunderstorm, the ever-
present mosquitoes might swell up into a swarm, transforming
themselves from a nuisance into a danger in an instant. Wind-
blown clouds of the little vampires descended on caravans in

such numbers and with such suddenness that man, woman and beast were covered within seconds. In the face of such an attack, people could do little but grab a blanket, dive under their carts and seal themselves within their hastily made woollen shelters. They spent awful moments waiting helplessly, often in the heat of high summer, while their writhing dogs yelped in agony and their terrified horses bucked wildly in their traces, screaming and whinnying until the swarm passed. Animals were sometimes lost to these ravenous swarms, and men might be disabled for days. At times, the caravans were warned by the awful hum of the advancing swarm, growing louder as it wafted across the plains, and the Métis quickly threw wagon sheets over their animals before taking cover to weather the insect storm. A horse's keen sense often detected the danger before the men did, and many an unprepared rider was unceremoniously dumped from the back of his spooked mount as a result.

The greatest danger on the plains, however, was the possibility of a Native attack. Throughout much of the early 18th century, the Métis were at odds with the ever-expanding and highly aggressive Sioux Confederacy over hunting grounds. Relations between Métis and Sioux fluctuated between flat-out hostility and tentative tolerance, but even at their best moments, the two groups maintained a constant vigilance. The relationship between these two peoples was born out of three generations of continuous mistrust and occasional bloodshed, and although they eventually formed tenuous alliances against eastern expansion, Métis and Sioux never completely reconciled the legacy of their forefathers.

"We lived in peace," Louis Goulet said of the Sioux during the last years of Sioux ascendancy, "but were always armed to the teeth."

Gabriel Dumont experienced the ire of the Sioux firsthand when he was still in adolescence. He was a mere 13 years old in the summer of 1851, when Isidore Dumont took the captaincy of the White Horse Plains Métis' hunting expedition, rather than the caravan departing a few miles east from Red River. The White Horse Plains caravan was smaller than the Red River caravan that year—about 300 people. Rumours abounded that the Sioux's patience with the Métis had reached a breaking point, and that they intended to do something about the people whom they regarded as interlopers on their traditional hunting grounds. The leaders of the Red River and White Horse Plains expeditions met before setting out, making plans to come to each other's aide should trouble arise with the Sioux.

So it was that the two creaking columns set out to the southwest in early June, travelling in parallel lines far enough apart not to interfere with each other's hunting, yet close enough to provide help in the event of a Sioux attack. As the White Horse Plains group approached the outer ridges of that rough country known as the Grand Coteau (Missouri), the Métis became even more cautious. The Grand Coteau is a great break in the prairie landscape that divides the Missouri and Assiniboine River basins. Centuries before, the earth here had been patiently wounded by the departing glaciers and it still bore the scars. The ground is a tumbled mess rising out of the plains, with hills, ridges and isolated buttes in abundance— a perfect place for an ambush.

Métis scouts rode a little farther ahead. Fully aware of the opportunity that the Grand Coteau presented their enemies, these scouts were ever more watchful, keeping their eyes peeled for any sign of human passage. The lead riders who ascended to the first high point of the Coteau must have felt a shudder of fear as their blinking eyes took in the sight that greeted them. Stretched out before them was the largest encampment of Teton Sioux any Métis had ever seen— 400–500 lodges with approximately 2500 warriors. The scouts quickly composed themselves and galloped back to the advancing Métis column, each of them issuing a silent prayer to a Christian God.

When the scouts reached the column, their horses' flanks foaming from the hard ride, they gave their report with ragged breath. The hunt's leader, Baptiste Falcon, listened in silence. He knew that a gathering so large was no accident. The Sioux were clearly on the warpath, determined to destroy any Métis interlopers they encountered, a fact that Falcon accepted with grim certainty.

He turned and sang out the order to the column behind him, *"Former le ronde!"*

The command was relayed down the line, rider to rider, and the straight wagon train slowly curved, turning in on itself, until all the Red River carts formed one enormous circle. Thus arranged, each rider quickly dismounted from his cart, unhitched his animals, tilted his wagon backwards on its two rear wheels, shafts jutting into the air and tied its wheels together with leather thongs to make them immobile. The men then set to work, furiously digging shallow trenches just behind the carts to shelter their families, while the women and children lashed the cart wheels together and gathered the livestock in the centre of the circle. After the trenches inside the circle were finished, the men ran about 60 yards from the carts and began digging a series of rifle pits from which they could defend the circle behind them. In a matter of minutes, the Métis wagon train became a veritable fortress.

In the meantime, a group of five hunters had volunteered to go forward and try to parley with the Sioux. Perhaps thinking that showing a bold hand might forestall violence, the five bravely, or in retrospect perhaps foolishly, advanced straight towards the huge Sioux camp in plain sight. A large group of braves under their war chieftain, White Horse, rode out to meet them. The five quickly found themselves surrounded and knew with one look at the braves' faces that no hope for a peaceful parley existed. Two of the Métis made a desperate break for freedom. Galloping between the Sioux lines and riding low on their fleet steeds to avoid the shots of their pursuers, these two made it back to the *ronde* in one piece. The Sioux captured three of their comrades—Jérome Magdalis, Baptiste Malaterre and James Whiteford.

Hot on the heels of the two escaping men, White Horse and his band of braves rode up until they were close enough to address the Métis.

"Listen to me, Slota," White Horse called out, addressing the Métis by the name the Lakota had given them. "You come every year onto the land of my people, with your horses and your carts, your women and children. You come and kill the buffalo, leaving always less for us. You are not welcome here any longer." White Horse gestured to the lands around him with one broad sweep of his thick arm, indicating that everything they saw belonged to the Sioux. "We will return at morning's first light to give you back your prisoners," the chief continued, "and will take any gifts the Slota offer." With that White Horse turned haughtily and rode off with his braves.

White Horse sounded conciliatory, but none of the Métis believed him. In 1851, relations between Sioux and Métis were far too sour for appeasement. Every man, woman and child in the *ronde* was convinced that a fight was imminent. And the prospect must have seemed daunting indeed. Their complement consisted of 64 hunters and just over a dozen boys that could handle a gun; 13-year-old Gabriel Dumont was among them. This modest group was up against more than 2000 determined Sioux warriors.

With their lumbering carts and their draft animals in tow, the Métis could hardly have hoped to escape. Neither was surrender an inviting option, given the torture and eventual death that most probably awaited prisoners captured in war. Their only choice was to stand and fight.

Isidore was at first unwilling to see his young son in the front lines of the rifle pits, but Gabriel stubbornly insisted on keeping his place, and because every hand that could handle a gun was so urgently needed, his father soon acquiesced. So it was that Métis boys hunkered down shoulder to shoulder with the men, ready to repel what they believed to be an inevitable attack.

Later that day, when three Natives rode nonchalantly towards the Métis camp, 10 hunters vaulted onto their chargers and galloped out to drive off the small party, assuming that the trio was there to inspect the Métis defences. The rest of the day wore on without further incident, and a tense silence descended over the circle of wagons. After sunset, two men rode out under cover of darkness to try and reach the Red River caravan to ask for desperately needed help. The hours passed slowly in the darkness of the nervous *ronde* that night.

Father Laflèche, the caravan's priest, said Mass and received the confessions of his imperilled congregation as the sky grew light on June 13. A fearsome spectacle, seen by few and survived by fewer, soon welcomed them into the new day. Hundreds upon hundreds of Sioux warriors rode towards them, in full war paint and dress, their war songs ringing out fierce and loud in the still morning air. The huge war party pulled up some distance from the *ronde*, and the Métis, showing no fear, rode out in a force of 30 strong to meet them.

What must have appeared a minuscule portion of the Sioux army broke off to meet the Métis halfway. White Horse rode at their head unarmed, except for the rattle in his hand and the defiant song on his lips, a boastful show of contempt for his adversaries. He brought in his wake the three prisoners captured the previous day. That was when a desperate Jérome Magdalis surprised his captors, making a sudden bid for escape as the two groups drew near. The intrepid man actually managed to break away from the contingent of Sioux horsemen, fuelled by mortal terror, running his horse to the safety of the wagons. He was obviously terrified by what he had experienced in the previous hours, and as he struggled to catch his breath, he warned his fellows not to trust the Sioux, who had spent the entire night in a war dance.

Still, the Métis tried to make peace. They offered gifts to White Horse and the other Sioux chieftains, asking the Natives to turn back and to let them pass. An indignant White Horse, his anger freshly piqued by Magdalis' escape from right under his nose, refused the olive branch. He declared that he had no need for negotiations because his braves could crush the small camp with ease, and he could then take what he desired. With that he waved his warriors forward.

Their brief parley now unquestionably over, the Métis turned their horses. Digging heels into flanks, they galloped back into the briefly opened *ronde* before the Sioux could cut them off. The leading hunters jumped off their horses and hit the ground running, on their way to reinforce the soon-to-be-besieged rifle pits.

All at once, the hills came to life with the fierce sound of a thousand battle whoops. And then the Sioux charged. Métis rifles instantly came to life within the *ronde*, felling the young chief who led the charge and dozens of others. The rifle fire was so devastatingly accurate that the mounted Sioux slowed, hesitated and then turned back. In the confused moments after the charge, when the Métis shouted jubilantly at the retreating enemy, the two remaining prisoners made a break for the circle of their people. Whiteford, on a fast horse, made good, but poor Malaterre could not keep up and was felled in the chase. Meaning to demoralize their Métis opponents, two braves rode up to Malaterre's corpse, sliced off parts of his body and held their gruesome trophies aloft on their spears.

For the rest of the day, the Sioux threatened the Métis constantly, making probing charges and engaging in skirmishes with the hunters who were well protected in their rifle pits.

Inside the *ronde*, several women grabbed spare muskets and fired at any brave that came too near the circle. Father Laflèche made his rounds of the improvised Métis fortress, holding his crucifix above his head as he urged the Métis to fight on, praying aloud and earnestly to his God for aid and strength. At his side, however, the good Father carried a hefty axe; he intended to go down swinging, if it came to it.

It did not. The Métis fought throughout the day. As the hot midsummer sun made its torturously sluggish arc across the prairie sky, the besieged hunters-turned-warriors shot at any good target that presented itself. Many of them had to go the whole day without food or water. Gabriel was one of the lucky few, however; his rifle pit had been braced with improvised sandbags of buffalo jerky. Years later he would joke that this provision allowed him to "eat the ramparts" throughout the day.

He fought as well as any of the full-fledged hunters. And it was on that day that Gabriel Dumont, barely in his teens, killed for the first time, shooting down a Sioux horseman who had ridden across his rifle site. Even as a strange heaviness grew in the pit of his stomach, he flushed with pride when one of the hunters clapped him on the shoulder.

"Good shot, Gabriel!"

In the late afternoon, the Sioux attempted another full-scale charge, but it was repulsed even more decidedly than the day's first attack. The numbers of their dead were mounting, and the Sioux were becoming demoralized. They had suffered many casualties, and their attacks on the stubborn Métis defenders seemed to have little effect. During one charge, a Sioux chief made it close enough to the *ronde* to make out Father Laflèche praying fervently with a group of women. The chief made it back to the Sioux position, where he announced his discovery.

"The wagon-men have a Manitou with them," he called out, referring to the spiritual aid of Father Laflèche. "That is why we cannot kill them." That was enough for the Sioux. Slowly but surely, some more eagerly than others, the Sioux retreated to their camp.

Thunderstorms blew in as evening darkened the sky, and a collective Métis council decided to break camp in the pre-dawn hours and retreat gingerly in the direction of the much larger Red River hunt. Thus, the morning sun of June 14 found the columns of carts crawling steadily across the rough terrain. They had been moving for only about an hour when one of the outlying scouts raced back into camp with the news that the Sioux were in pursuit. Again, the cry rang out, *"Former le ronde!"* and again, the Métis speedily transformed their caravan into a fort.

The Sioux wasted little time, charging the little Métis stronghold shortly after they arrived. The battle proceeded in similar fashion as it had the day before. The air was filled with the sound of charging horses, the whooping of fiercely painted Sioux braves, the flash and crack of muskets, songs of war and cries of pain. Métis and Sioux clashed repeatedly for five hours in ever-intensifying skirmishes. As the fighting continued, however, storm clouds again gathered across the sky. The Sioux made a last concerted effort to overwhelm their Métis foe, riding in fast and close to the *ronde*, firing and whooping wildly as they enveloped the enclosure. But the determined Métis again held their ground and turned back the almost inexorable charge. Once again, young Gabriel was in the thick of the fight.

Later that evening, amid the pouring rain, hunters from the Red River group rode into the relieved camp, bringing with them 300 Salteaux Natives, long-standing enemies of the Sioux. The increased numbers effectively discouraged the Sioux from any more attacks. If they had been unable to defeat a tiny force of 70 Métis in two days of fighting, they certainly didn't feel confident about testing themselves against a force roughly 10 times larger.

Thus ended one of the most famous battles in Métis history and one of their most impressive victories. They had faced odds of more than 20 to 1 and won. Not only that, but aside from the unfortunate Malaterre, only three Métis were wounded in the two days of fighting, one of whom was Isidore Dumont. The Sioux suffered 80 dead, and their total casualties were probably much higher. Young Gabriel's part had been relatively minor, although still courageous for an untried teenager. Thirty years hence, Gabriel Dumont would play a much more commanding role in Métis victories and one well-known defeat. But many cycles of frozen winters and summer hunts would pass before these famous events would come to pass.

CHAPTER THREE

A New Way of Living

*"There were no more herds like those
I remember seeing."*

THE MÉTIS CULTURE FLOURISHED AS long as buffalo herds covered
the Plains, but the era of the great hunts was doomed to end. At
the beginning of the 1800s, an estimated 50–60 million buffalo roamed the western plains. European travellers throughout
the West in the late 18th century were awed by the sight of these
herds; many wrote home about the incredible numbers, vast
contiguous packs that took days to ride through. By 1830, the
population had already declined to approximately 30 million.
But there were still years of plenty. The Métis hunts still yielded
a bountiful harvest in 1840. Just enough buffalo remained to
maintain the illusion that the herds and the way of life they
sustained might last forever.

But the illusion was fading fast. Already in 1862, British
adventurers Lord Milton and Dr. Walter Cheadle reported a
noticeable decline: "The buffalo have receded so far from the
forts, and the quantity of whitefish from the lakes, one of

the principal sources of supply, has decreased so greatly, that a winter rarely passes without serious suffering from want of food...The days when it was possible to live in plenty by the gun and net alone, have already gone by on the North Saskatchewan." By the 1870s, those dependent upon the bison for sustenance fell on hard times, and by 1879, the buffalo had almost vanished entirely from Canadian territory.

Why was this? The answer was simple—humans. Various Native tribes of the Plains had hunted the buffalo in different ways for centuries; some of these methods were quite destructive. Thousands were stampeded off cliffs, such as those at present-day Head-Smashed-In Buffalo Jump, west of Fort Macleod, Alberta. Entire herds were driven into prepared stockades—a technique probably seen by Gabriel in his youthful travels across the West—which would lock shut behind the last animal, whereupon a great slaughter of the trapped beasts would take place.

But the intensity of the overall slaughter was increased with the ever-greater number of white men who arrived in the region. The introduction of guns and the fur trade into the West was partly responsible. The trade created a thriving market for parts of the buffalo—skins, furs and the like— while the production of pemmican allowed traders to penetrate deeper into the West in pursuit of more furs. Buffalo were killed en masse, their over-abundance encouraging wastefulness. Hunters often killed them only for their most valuable parts, while leaving the rest of the carcasses for the wolves and coyotes.

A scale that had been in equilibrium for centuries began to be pushed out of balance. An increasing human population was making greater demands on the shrinking buffalo herds. As buffalo stocks declined under these ever-increasing pressures, they became less and less able to replenish themselves and rebound from the mass killings. In the 1870s, the last few million bison were exterminated with a swiftness that surprised nearly everyone.

Louis Goulet, a contemporary of Gabriel Dumont, recalled the heartbreaking disappearance of the buffalo:

> By the time I was six or eight years old, it was between 1865 and 1870, and the Red River country had already changed a lot. For the past couple of years the buffalo had been nothing but a memory of days gone by. There were no more herds like those I remembered seeing in the valley. Quite a few little boys my age had never even set eyes on one of those proud animals. We had just seen proof that the old-timers were wrong in thinking that the immense herds could never be wiped out.

She was a fine comely woman.

Gabriel Dumont was a man whose life straddled this period of transition, stretching back from the golden age of the Métis' and forward into very different times. After the Battle of Grand Coteau, no Métis hunter treated Gabriel like a child. His unflinching bravery in the face of the Sioux attack ensured his place among them. At the age of 13, Gabriel Dumont took his place in the buffalo runs. The 1850s marched on, and the Dumonts continued to hunt, travel and trade. Gabriel's childhood days were slipping through his fingers like sand, but it is doubtful that the robust adolescent was sad to put his youth behind him. Gabriel Dumont was all too eager to embrace adulthood along with all the responsibilities it entailed. And the end of the decade brought a series of events that washed away what little innocence Gabriel still had.

In 1858, a terrible smallpox epidemic ravaged the people of the prairies. These outbreaks were horrific occurrences, the worst killing 30 of every 100 people infected. Generally, the first

The killing of buffalo for sport contributed to the decimation of the herds and the collapse of the Native and Métis cultures dependent on the buffalo

symptoms were chills, headache, backache, nausea, vomiting and fever, seeming at first like the flu or a bad cold. But after a few days, red spots appeared on the face and arms, spreading to the torso and the legs. The fever persisted, and the spots became raised. In a few days, the spots became angry blisters filled with pus that swelled agonizingly. If the patient lived, the blisters dried up, the fever dropped and the person's condition began to improve. Scabs formed and eventually dropped off, often leaving red or brown discolorations. If the eruptions were severe, pockmarks remained on the unfortunate person's skin.

In the fear that accompanied the epidemic, many prairie inhabitants separated from the greater community to avoid becoming infected. Small groups of immediate families headed off into the wilderness, living off the land as best they could in relative isolation. As they ran from one scourge, however, another struck the Dumont family. Gabriel's mother, Louise, died of consumption.

These days were sad and sobering for the young man, who soon began a family of his own. In a humble ceremony celebrated by Father Joseph Goiffon, a French missionary, in the small Métis village of St. Joseph, just south of the border in Dakota, Gabriel took as his bride young Madeleine Wilkie. He was 21 years old.

Politically, the union was an intelligent move. Madeleine was the daughter of the influential Métis hunt leader Jean-Baptiste Wilkie, and the wedding bound the two powerful families together. If the pairing was conceived as a political move, it soon evolved into something more. A bond of genuine affection developed between Madeleine and Gabriel. To their regret, they were never able to have children, but they adopted a child named Annie from the Red River region.

John Kerr, who worked for Gabriel a little over a decade later, could not help but notice the prevailing harmony in the Dumont household: "In his own home Gabriel was never quarrelsome, and his wife and adopted daughter never got an unkind word from him." Dumont's family life was the envy of his friends, although both Gabriel and Madeleine regretted that they were unable to have any children of their own.

Relatively little is known of Madeleine. Kerr described her as "a fine comely woman," adding, with a nudge and a wink, that "people often wondered what she saw in such a homely chap as Gabriel—for he was homely." Madeleine was tough, as Métis women had to be, hefting heavy sacks of pemmican and heading off to Winnipeg to sell Gabriel's furs and skins without a second thought, while he led the summer buffalo hunts. She had an advantage in trading because, unlike Gabriel, she could speak English. She has been described as a pious, compassionate woman, imbued with a profound understanding of the importance of community in the face of a hard environment. Madeleine made it her business to assist any Métis in need, a quality she shared with her generous husband.

Gabriel's hard frontier education made him into the man that he was; it thickened his skin, sharpened his instincts and killed his sentimentalism. Yet his passage through adolescence also cultivated a streak of generosity for which Dumont became famous. Madeleine was the chief beneficiary of Dumont's open-handedness. In 1859, he purchased a substantial £10 worth of goods from Lower Fort Garry, the bulk of which was for his wife. He brought her back yards of various types of material, a generous supply of ribbon, thimbles and needles, which Madeleine no doubt put to good use in brightening her home and wardrobe. Later, when the couple became more established, Gabriel also bought her a foot-powered washing machine to ease her chores—a machine that surely made Madeleine the envy of many a Métis wife.

The young couple witnessed some dramatic changes to the traditional Métis way of life. Eastern technology flooded into the North-West. Where Métis fathers managed without iron implements, half a generation later, their sons could not imagine life without them. Hammers, augers, saws, screws and nails quickly became part of everyday life in Gabriel's time. Metal fasteners and iron bolts replaced wooden pegs and traditional wedge construction. Industrial technology reached into the hinterlands to reshape the Métis way of life.

And just as metal seeped into the West, so too did many Métis begin shifting to a more sedentary lifestyle. More and more were raising livestock, and almost every family began practising some form of agriculture. Many Métis limited their activities to modest vegetable gardens, but ever-increasing numbers were sowing small fields of wheat, oats and barley. The dwindling buffalo herds that caused the ever-waning bounty of the hunt was replaced a little more each year with agricultural practice. Many were greatly disturbed by the shift that they perceived to be the erosion of an established way of life. The buffalo disappeared so quickly that most adult Métis could remember the not-too-distant time of the great buffalo hunts, and they greeted the new, more settled ways with no small amount of dissatisfaction.

But many grudgingly accepted the changes and tried to adapt to them as best they could while remaining in Red River, which became too far removed from the dwindling buffalo herds to be a centre for the great hunts. Others still refused to give up the traditional ways and moved farther west and north to where the buffalo still roamed in number. Gabriel and his generation of the Dumonts were among the Métis who chose to follow the buffalo.

Eventually, a group of about 200 Métis hunters based themselves and their families in an area near Fort Carlton, just south of the North Saskatchewan River in what is now central Saskatchewan. In 1863, at the unusually young age of 25, Dumont was chosen as the leader of the hunt, a position he held every year until 1880 when the buffalo hunt died out completely. But Dumont's responsibilities to his people did not end with the hunt. It wasn't long before the skilled young hunter, tough, resourceful and generous, proved himself to be an able leader away from the hunt as well, carving out a place for himself and his people along the North Saskatchewan. It was at this time that Gabriel's character, which was lent weight by his extraordinary acts of courage and magnanimity, began to take on the aspect of legend. Métis and Native, ally and enemy alike respected him.

Fort Carlton, established in 1810 as an HBC fur-trading post and burned to the ground during the North-West Rebellion of 1885

One account has Dumont leading a modest group of six hunters and their families on a small-scale hunting trip. They were making their way towards the hunting grounds when they came upon a large encampment of Cree. Traditional allies of the Métis, the Cree did not think anything of it when Gabriel's group pitched camp next to them, using it as their base of operations for the hunt.

The first few days passed uneventfully enough, with Gabriel and the hunters going about their work during the day while their women stayed behind, tending to the work around camp. The Cree were holding a war council to plan an attack on their traditional enemy, the Blackfoot. None paid the small group of Métis any mind, leaving them to go about their business. That all changed when a single Cree brave barged into the Dumont tent unannounced, intent on getting something for nothing.

Gabriel and the other men were off hunting, and Madeleine was alone.

A startled Madeleine took only a moment to compose herself. "What are you doing in my tent, stranger?" she asked the intruder, speaking in Cree and staring him straight in the face.

The brave looked irritated at having to explain himself, and his response was stern. "My people are about to go to war against the Blackfoot, woman. We need all the best horses in the camp."

He was telling Madeleine the truth. The warrior had been walking throughout the camp, looking out for battle-ready mounts when his eyes fell on the animals chained up outside the Métis camp. He was especially drawn to one magnificent roan that looked like it could be the finest animal in the camp. This was the animal he was after.

"A woman has no use for that brown animal," he said, nodding his head at Gabriel's favourite horse, which was just visible through the tent flap.

"That horse doesn't belong to me," Madeleine replied. "It is the horse of Gabriel Dumont, my husband. If you take it, he will not be happy."

The man was unimpressed by her warning. "Woman, if you don't unlock that animal, I will kill it where it stands. Will this make your husband happy?"

Madeleine could tell the warrior wasn't bluffing and decided that it would be best to unlock Gabriel's horse.

"I warn you," Madeleine said to the brave, as she loosened the chains, "my husband will not let this pass."

The Cree grabbed the reins and rode off without a word.

That evening when Dumont returned, he immediately noticed that his horse was missing, as he was tying up the courser he had used for the day's hunting. The first thing that flashed through his mind was Madeleine. He dashed into the tent, anxious at the thought that something might have happened to her. Gabriel calmed somewhat when he saw that his wife was unharmed, but there was still the matter of the horse. Madeleine told him what had transpired, and Gabriel, his heart thudding against his ribs like an angered beast, made straight for the Cree camp.

He found the Cree braves in the centre of the camp, in the midst of a war dance. Dumont knew the Cree and their customs well and knew that protocol would not allow him to interrupt such an important ceremony. He reined in his anger and waited silently in the main lodge among the Cree women. But as soon as the dancing was finished, Dumont charged out into the group of surprised braves and demanded to be heard.

In the time that he had spent waiting, Gabriel's reason had caught up with his anger, and when he addressed the braves before him, it was with a calm and steady voice.

"Friends," he called out, his deep voice rolling over the gathered men. "Most of you here know who I am and know of my people, just as our fathers knew one another and lived together in peace." It was a strange thing for a man to be talking about peace right after a war dance, and the Cree glared at Gabriel Dumont in silence, unsure what to think.

"We are like brothers, the Métis and the Cree, and I have always sworn to stand by my brothers in front of their enemy. Tomorrow, you go to fight the Blackfoot; this is good. I will go and fight beside you and show you by my courage, my strength and my skill that I am the best of any man who rides a horse and shoots a rifle."

Gabriel paused as he held the camp's undivided attention. It was the custom for warriors to brag about their skill and their accomplishments the night before a battle, but the Cree saw something different about the sturdy Métis man standing before them. It may have been the way he stood, the complete self-assurance of his stance, his natural command over the men around him, the way his eyes flashed as he addressed his Cree audience. He was a formidable physical presence, and even though he stood no taller than 5'9", Gabriel's massive shoulders, thick neck and heavily muscled limbs lent him an impression of enormousness.

"But even though I will fight with my brothers, today you have done something to offend me." Gabriel's eyes went from one brave to the next. "When I wasn't even there, you took my horse. It was not brave to scare my wife. Since I married her we have always been together, and what is done to my wife is done to me." His look was an open challenge to those around him. He finished with steely resolve. "I will not let it pass."

One of the Cree elders who knew something of Gabriel Dumont's reputation among his people stood up to speak.

"My son," the old man began, "I have heard the stories about your rifle and your kinship with horses. I know you are a good man, a chief of your people." Dumont received the address in silence. "But you must know that the man who took your horse did not mean to offend you or scare your wife. It is customary that friends and allies give us their best mounts when we go to war. It is Cree law."

"I do not follow your law," Dumont responded, cutting off the elder. Gabriel could have stopped here and probably returned to his tent with his horse, but he knew that bigger issues were in play than a single horse. Young Dumont was an ambitious man, and he was intent on demonstrating his superiority over the fighting men surrounding him.

"If you want me to go to war with you," Dumont said, his voice a low rumble, "there will be no one before me when we ride against the enemy. I will be the first man here to meet the Blackfoot." A murmur spread through the crowd. "I swear that I will strike down the first man tomorrow. If I do not keep my word, you can keep my horse, for I would blush to own that fine animal. But as long as I am always first to go up against the enemy," Dumont said, his voice rising, "then nobody should touch my horses when I am not there."

And so it was that the following day Dumont rode out across the prairie, the lone Métis at the head of a Cree war party set on a collision course with a party of Blackfoot braves. The two groups pulled up when they were a few hundred yards apart. The men stopped and appraised the strength of the other side, covered in war paint and bellowing their songs of battle. The Blackfoot shouted threats and strutted, brandished their weapons and eagerly professed their fearlessness. The din of imminent battle had just reached its pitched crescendo when a lone Blackfoot charged forward. Halfway towards the Cree, he halted and sang a war song, laying bare his courage for all to see, taunting the Cree.

Knowing that the trial of the previous evening's words had arrived, Dumont charged down on the lone brave. The brave turned to gallop back to his own line, but Gabriel had chosen his next best steed and quickly overtook the warrior, galloping alongside the fleeing Native and forcing him to change direction. A desperate chase ensued, the riders zigzagging away from the two groups of Natives. Dumont kept his cool, matching every turn the warrior made until he was right on the panicked brave. The riders were close enough to touch when Dumont pulled his rifle from its holster, jammed the muzzle against the man's chest and fired. Dead in a split second, the Blackfoot warrior toppled from his horse, a spray of blood tracing his fall. Dumont grabbed the bridle of the riderless pony and galloped it back to the Cree lines. It was all over in seconds, but Dumont took no pride in what he'd done. His first thought was to return and check on the Blackfoot. Dumont could clearly see that the man was dead. In the coming years, when he would tell this story to his fellow Métis around night fires, Dumont would express his regret at the death of the brave young man.

"He was dead, and that made me sad," Gabriel said, "because the man had never done me any harm." Nevertheless, whatever reservations he had against murder, Dumont succeeded in what he set out to do—win his horse back and secure his reputation among the Cree braves.

He was Bull Hide, a grand chief of his nation.

Another tale from Gabriel's life that added to his legendary status took place somewhere in the middle of the prairie. Dumont was out by himself, patrolling the lands around his settlement when he spotted a lone rider on the prairie. Gabriel quickly made out that the man was a Blood. The Métis had no standing peace arrangement with the Blood, but neither were the two peoples at war. Nevertheless, the code of the prairie dictated that every man should put up a strong face for his tribe, and so the two men spurred their horses and charged headlong at each other with blood-curdling whoops and cries, each convinced that the other would be the first to turn his bridle.

For a few frantic moments, this game of frontier chicken looked as if it might end in the demise of both riders. But when they were mere yards from each other, the Blood warrior lost his nerve and swerved from Dumont's path. That was when Gabriel, young and cocky, decided to press the issue. He noted that the Blood was only armed with a bow and arrow, which he had not yet been able to draw. Meaning to unhorse the man, Gabriel pulled his horse up next to the galloping Blood until the animals were running shoulder to shoulder. Gabriel then stood up in his stirrups, swung one leg over his saddle and jumped onto the brave's horse. Landing behind the Native, Dumont wrapped his arms around the astonished Blood and grabbed hold of the reins. The Native, locked in Gabriel's vice-like grip, could only sit helplessly as Dumont guided the horse back to the Métis camp.

When they arrived, the Native, who probably feared he would be made a prisoner and possibly tortured to death, as was a common practice among some Plains Natives, was surprised when

Dumont produced some tobacco and a pipe. This was a gesture of peace and goodwill on the open prairie. The brave smoked the pipe, but unable to fully accept his good fortune or shake his uneasiness, he refused to dismount. When they finished the tobacco, Dumont smiled heartily at the young brave.

"I did not mean any harm; I was only out for a bit of fun," Dumont said. "You can go now."

The Blood didn't have to be told twice and galloped away as fast as his horse would carry him. Gabriel looked on the retreating man with a broad grin, knowing that he had accomplished his purpose. Eventually, the stunt would pay tremendous dividends.

About 20 years later, when Gabriel had long been the acknowledged leader of the Métis, he made a trip into Blood territory, hoping to negotiate peace. He recognized the brave the instant he saw him. He was older, with long white strands mingled in his black locks, but Gabriel did not doubt that he was the same Blood with whom he had smoked tobacco so many years ago. The Blood recognized him too, smiling widely when Gabriel rode into their camp. It turned out that the man whom he'd bested and whose deep respect he'd earned two decades earlier was none other than Bull Hide, one of the most respected chiefs of his nation. Gabriel had no problem negotiating peace with the Blood.

The Red River Rebellion

Such feats had made Gabriel a living Métis legend by the time the troubles broke out on the Red River. By 1869, this easternmost Métis settlement had grown to become the largest in the North-West, inhabited by about 10,000 of Gabriel's countrymen. But the Métis who lived on the Red River were very different from those who lived under Gabriel Dumont's leadership farther west in the Saskatchewan valley. While

Gabriel's people still clung to the ways of the buffalo hunt, the Red River Métis had learned to accept that the buffalo were gone, taking on the sedentary ways of the European settler, supporting themselves on agriculture and domesticated cattle. It was a difficult transition, made all the more so by the easterners who were moving onto their lands.

In the spring of 1869, a mere two years after Confederation, the Canadian government arranged a deal for the purchase of that immense sweep of land then "owned," at least on paper, by the Hudson's Bay Company. But no one, however, had bothered to consult the people who actually lived in Rupert's Land. The Red River Métis were particularly concerned.

Throughout the 1860s, English-Canadian immigrants had started trickling into the area in greater numbers, and they did not leave a favourable impression. Indeed, these early *émigrés* from Ontario, most of them virulent Protestant Orangemen, opposed anyone or anything related to the established order in the region. They railed against the Hudson's Bay Company, the Catholic Church and anyone who had the audacity to speak French in their presence.

The Red River Métis grew understandably anxious in the face of this first wave of Canadian settlers. Residents of a land that was about to be purchased by the Canadian government, were the Métis to be deprived of any say in their fate? What would happen to their language, culture and religion under Canadian governance? What of their homes, their narrow land lots surveyed in the French fashion? The system did not correspond to the planned Canadian scheme of square quarter-mile sections and therefore was not recognized by Canadian law. These questions remained unanswered while discontent and anxiety grew.

In August 1869, a Canadian government survey party began to mark out the square lots in the Red River region. A young and well-educated Métis named Louis Riel, who was

A photograph of Louis Riel's closest advisers, taken in 1869. *Top row, left to right:* Charles Larocque, Pierre Delorme, Thomas Bunn, Xavier Pagée, Ambroise Lépine, Baptiste Tourond, Thomas Spence. *Middle row:* Pierre Pointras, John Bruce, Louis Riel, William B. O'Donoghue, Françoise Dauphinais. *Front row:* H.F. O'Lone, Paul Proulx. John Bruce, seated on Louis' right, was the presidential figurehead of the National Committee, but dropped off the political map after he contracted a serious illness. When he recuperated, the former committee president found that there was no spot set aside for him in the new provisional government. He never forgave Louis Riel for this perceived slight.

destined to play a major role in Canadian history and in Gabriel Dumont's life, spoke out publicly against these surveys. Riel acted as a lightning rod for the discontent that was rife in the region. On October 11, when the survey crew tried to survey through a Métis farm, they found Riel and a gang of scowling Métis riders standing in their way. Riel soon became a leading member of the Métis National Committee, an organized governing force acting as a voice of dissent against Canadian ambitions in Red River.

This National Committee barred the appointed lieutenant-governor from entering the region and seized Fort Garry, an act that the fort's Hudson's Bay Company officials wisely did not resist. In the unrest that followed, the alarmed Canadian government asked the British government to delay the transfer of the North-West indefinitely. The authority of the Hudson's Bay Company in the region, however, still came to an end on December 1, which meant that the territory now had no formal government at all. A provisional government was proclaimed on December 10, 1869, and two weeks later, Riel was chosen as its president.

News of these actions caused quite a stir, in the West and throughout the country and beyond. Word of the Red River resistance quickly spread across the prairie, reaching Dumont and his people on the South Saskatchewan before the year was up. Dumont staunchly supported the Red River movement and did not hesitate to send Louis Riel a message, pledging the service of 500 horsemen under his command.

Meanwhile, from the perspective of Riel and the Red River Métis, things were progressing well back at Fort Garry. The Canadian government, having no army to speak of and no way to get a military force to Fort Garry in the middle of winter even if it had, admitted that it had no alternative but to negotiate with Riel's provisional government. The Canadian government sent three ambassadors to Fort Garry to do just

Thomas Scott's execution sent tremors of fear and rage into English-speaking Ontario. Scott became a martyr, Riel a fugitive.

that. A committee consisting of most of the English settlers and the Métis was able to reach a rough agreement and collectively determined a "List of Rights," which was to be sent back to Ottawa with the three Canadian envoys as the basis for negotiating Red River's entry into Confederation. Delegates from Red River followed soon after, and despite a mounting and vociferous protest in Ontario, Parliament speedily passed a bill that fairly represented Red River's List of Rights into law as the Manitoba Act. The resistance, with Riel at its head, had been successful.

The opposition in Ontario, however, was galvanized by one serious miscalculation on Riel's part. Some of the English Canadians in Red River refused to recognize the provisional government and organized an armed resistance. One of these men, the notoriously obnoxious Thomas Scott, was captured, held in jail, tried by the provisional government and executed by firing squad on March 4, 1870. His death provided a martyr to those back East who were opposed to negotiating with Riel's provisional government and who wished to inflame public opinion against the Métis. Worse, Thomas Scott had been a member of the powerful Orange Order, a staunchly, almost militant pro-British and Protestant organization. The order railed against the Roman Catholic Riel and asked for justice to be done for what they saw as the murder of Scott.

In the spring of 1870, the Canadian government sent a small military expedition composed of two militia battalions and one regiment of British regulars to Red River. The expedition was ostensibly to be "a mission of peace." It was also intended to provide a presence of authority to support the new lieutenant-governor, who was sent separately, in an effort to emphasize that this expedition was not a military takeover of Red River. It was quietly understood, however, that the endeavour was meant to appease the continuing furore in Ontario. With nothing other than verbal assurances that he would be granted amnesty for leading the resistance, Riel nervously fled Fort Garry as the troops neared it on August 24.

One Scow, the Best on the River

The events of that winter drifted into the past, although they were far from forgotten. Life along the North Saskatchewan rolled along. What was Dumont's life like during these years? It was around this time, in the early 1870s, that a youthful adventurer named John Kerr befriended Dumont. Kerr, who worked and lived with Dumont for years, was fascinated with the Métis patriarch and remembered him in vivid detail. He described him as looking "older than his age, which had barely reached the middle 30s," and having "rough-hewn features, an ungainly figure, and a scraggly beard." Kerr also noted the illusion of physical enormity that Gabriel possessed; people often described Gabriel as gigantic in stature, although he barely stood at medium height. Kerr attributed this impression to the breadth of Gabriel's shoulders and his heavy muscularity.

When Kerr first arrived in the region, the Métis leader was kind enough to take the young man in.

"I slept in Gabriel Dumont's tent," Kerr recounts. "It was through the intimacy thereby engendered, during that fall and the succeeding year, that I grew to know and respect the redoubtable Gabriel—chief outstanding figure of the Plains. To me he was kindness itself. He adopted me into his family and never called me by the name bestowed upon me by the rest of his band, namely *le Petit Canada* (*Petit* referred to my age, for I had height) but invariably addressed me as *mon frère*, while his family and relatives called me son, nephew, cousin and so forth, and I spoke to them in similar terms. Dumont has been painted in lurid colours as a savage, brutal man. He was anything but that, kindly and generous to a degree."

If Dumont looked older than his years, it may have been the responsibilities of leadership that he had carried from an early age, and carried well. Dumont did his best to care for and provide for his people. When there was trouble, the

river
it to
to
boil-

the
our
hich
own

inter
er to

been
the
with
tain
tarts
k of
the

for
A.
t to

porating himself as Bishop of Saskatchewan.
June 5, 1880.

45

NOTICE.

Gabriel's Crossing.

The public are informed that GABRIEL'S
Crossing is now in readiness for the accommodation of the public.

One Scow, the Best on the River,

will be in constant readiness. The road by
this ferry is the SHORTEST by twenty-five
miles going to or going east from Battleford.

The public promptly attended to.

GABRIEL DUMONT.

May, 1880.

45

Notice for the opening of Gabriel's Crossing and Dumont's ferry
carried in the *Saskatchewan Herald*, May 1880

community called on Gabriel. He acted as a rough and ready
doctor and sometime veterinarian on the Plains. He resolved
disputes, and his word carried the weight of law among the
Saskatchewan Métis.

Dumont was also quite able to take care of himself. He kept a
finger in many different pots, economically speaking. In the early
1870s he opened a ferry service that transported people heading

up the Fort Carlton trail across the South Saskatchewan—"One Scow, the Best on the River," as it was advertised. The business became an instrument of Gabriel's generosity. While he was away, conducting business or hunting, Gabriel made sure to employ the poor among the Métis to help Madeleine run things at what came to be known as "Gabriel's Crossing." One man, Isidore, was so poor that he did not even own a horse or a cart. When Gabriel heard that Isidore's wife had given birth, he immediately selected a horse from his stables and took it over to the man. He then returned to top off this already generous gift with a Red River cart filled with provisions.

Dumont also negotiated other means of employment for his people. In the 1870s, as the buffalo hunt grew leaner, Dumont arranged a contract with the Fort Carlton Hudson's Bay Company factor, Lawrence Clarke, for the Métis to construct a road from the fort to Green Lake. The men were paid $3 a day, and Dumont, who was in charge, slightly more.

"We made good headway on that road," John Kerr recalled. "Those Half-breeds *did* work, believe me, and no short days either. We made bridges over several small streams and gullies, clearing a road 12 feet wide, burning the brush and piling the logs at the side of the road whence they could easily be hauled to the fort for firewood."

Kerr acted as one of the camp's cooks, which, given the vegetable and animal scarcity of the Plains at the time, didn't allow for much culinary creativity. It was the season just prior to the buffalo hunt, and things were a little lean so the menu invariably included pemmican. Gabriel took pity on his men and resolved to do something about it.

One day, when the men were off working, Gabriel approached Kerr and said, "I go seek some bear meat, *mon frère*. Will you come too?" Kerr fairly jumped at the chance. Shortly, Gabriel tracked down a group of four bears. The two brought back enough bear meat for that day and for many days after.

The bear steaks were delicious, a welcome respite from the steady ration of greasy pemmican. Gabriel, however, did not just use the meat for the benefit of the work gang. Some of the best cuts found their way to the St. Laurent parish, where Gabriel lived, to those Métis who were too old or too young for hunting or working.

Gabriel looked after his people, but there was more to the man than skill with a rifle and an altruistic spirit. The Métis leader had a great sense of fun. He went to the trouble of ship-ping a billiard table to his store at the ferry crossing. With the addition of the billiard table, the store soon doubled as a sort of pub. Gabriel's Crossing became a popular gathering place, especially during the long winter nights, when the Métis for-gave the cramped quarters and short cues at Gabriel's store for some company, home brew and tobacco.

Another social occasion was the return of families and friends from their summer wanderings in preparation for winter. Such reunions often caused rowdy revelries that could last for weeks. Being one of the most successful Métis in his settlement, Gabriel was expected to supply much of the food and liquor for these parties, a task that the expert huntsman took on with zeal. And Gabriel's store quickly became the setting for most of the celebrations.

Legendary romps that rivalled any western hoe-down, these wild reunions were driven by the Métis' competitive spirit. Everything was a contest. The women competed for the biggest, most elaborate dishes, and the men challenged each other to drinking contests, and who could sing loudest, dance longest, even eat the most.

The mad cavorting was set to the cacophony of lively music that was made with instruments both traditional and impro-vised. Players bowed their fiddles, banged on drums or strummed guitars, while others beat wooden spoons together, slapped thighs, clapped hands or beat pots together. Any

The Métis were a fun-loving, passionate people. They took any excuse to dance and sing.

melody was eventually lost to the dominant beat, which grew more and more prominent as dancers banged their feet in time. If they were partying in a house with a wooden floor, the sound of pounding feet grew so loud that it could be heard 100 yards away. If it was a dirt floor, the dust kicked up by all the stamping got so bad that the revellers were often forced outside for air.

Another popular pastime was gambling. Gabriel, one of the more fervent gamblers in the Saskatchewan valley, hosted many gaming sessions in his store. So fervently did Métis men gamble, that winter sessions often went on for weeks. They put almost as much stock in a man's skill at the card table as they did in a man's skill with his rifle. Given that these hunters' work consisted of continuous, calculated risk-taking, in which a man's judgement was constantly being tested, the Métis' thrill for gambling makes sense. Thus the hunters' instinct embedded in all these men drove them to gamble on almost everything. They placed wagers on cards, on billiard games, on physical contests and on the weather. But they were especially taken with horse races. The Métis loved their horses and took great pride in their speed. Races between men's most prized animals could spring up with a single boastful word. All it took was one man's mention of the incredible fleetness of his animal for every man in earshot to throw down his wager. No Métis hunter worth his salt would let such a challenge go unanswered.

Another popular gambling event was similar to a prairie shell game. It consisted of a blanket, at least two different objects and two people. One man hid the objects under the blanket, the other guessed which was where, and the blanket was then removed to see if he had guessed correctly. The game, apparently, was as much psychological as anything else, with each man trying to intimidate the other, making a great show of his hiding or guessing. Others gathered around for the excitement and to bet on the proceedings.

This game also occasioned one of Dumont's more touching acts of generosity. Dumont had taken a visiting Cree brave badly at the blanket game, and when the poor fellow returned to his teepee, he suffered the double misfortune of falling gravely ill. When Dumont learned of the man's illness, he and Madeleine loaded up a sled with smoked buffalo meat, pemmican and medicine and delivered the much-needed supplies to the brave and his starving family. The grateful man later tried to repay Dumont by offering him his most prized buffalo robe, but Dumont graciously refused.

The people elected Dumont president...

Settlement crept inexorably westward, bringing change to the region. In 1871, a man named Xavier Letendre set up a store and ferry a little upstream from Gabriel's place. Xavier was nicknamed "Batoche," and his establishment became known as Batoche's Crossing and then simply Batoche. In 1874, a store opened at nearby Duck Lake, followed by a mission in 1876.

For Gabriel, however, one of the most important developments occurred in 1868—the arrival of Father Alexis André. Père André was a burly Breton, a salt-of-the-earth, no-nonsense preacher who looked more like a buffalo hunter than a man of the cloth. These were the very qualities, which provoked scorn and condescension from the more cultivated back East, that stood him well on the frontier and endeared him to the unpretentious Métis. André quickly won the trust and friendship of the community's most important resident, Gabriel Dumont.

In 1871, André settled among Gabriel's Métis and established a mission at St. Laurent. André, like other priests before him, did his best to encourage the Métis to adopt a more sedentary agricultural life. Priests tending to a settled flock found their work that much easier, but the reasons for encouraging settlement were not entirely selfish. Many priests, Father André among them, genuinely believed that established sedentary communities might be the only way to preserve the Métis culture against the incoming waves of immigrants.

Gabriel could see these changes happening around him, and he adapted. He had moved west in the 1860s to avoid the more settled life, but he was unable to avoid agriculture entirely, resorting to some small-scale farming—potatoes and barley—to make up for the ever-waning buffalo. By the early 1870s, Gabriel had come to accept that the buffalo were disappearing; he knew that another move farther west would provide little relief. Thus, Father André was able to convince the Métis leader to try a new path.

On December 10, 1873, Gabriel called for a meeting outside the doors of the church at St. Laurent. Dumont presided over the assembly, and Father André acted as secretary. The Métis of the St. Laurent region had decided that the loose summertime organization of the buffalo hunt would no longer suit their needs in a more settled community and so, on a frigid winter day in front of the church steps, they debated a new, more permanent type of government.

The people elected Dumont president by acclamation and chose a supporting council. The governing body enacted laws addressing its power and limitations, basic laws for the community and punishments for crimes. In February 1874, Dumont called another meeting to get a community consensus on laws regarding land as property. This action reflected the changing nature of life in the region; a decade earlier such laws would simply not have been required.

On December 10 of the following year, the community met again. They upheld the council and its decisions and again elected their unquestioned leader, Gabriel Dumont by acclamation. The council also passed more laws, again reflecting the changing realities of life in the West. The main issue tackled this time was not land, but the buffalo. The community upheld the traditional rules of the buffalo hunt, but in recognition of the alarming decline of the beasts, made the rules more stringent. For the first time, the wasteful practice of killing a buffalo and leaving its carcass for scavengers was made a crime.

But these laws were to bring about the dissolution of the promising but short-lived experiment in self-government. In contravention of the laws of their own community, a small group of Métis rode out before the main hunt began. With the smaller buffalo herds now on the prairies, the offence was considered serious, making the hunting that much more difficult for those who came behind. Dumont first had a letter drafted commanding the renegades to return to the fold of the hunt. When they didn't respond, Gabriel gathered together 40 men and rode down the maverick hunters. He imposed stiff fines of property and money on these men who, in the eyes of their fellows, were clearly criminals.

The renegades were not content to let the matter lie, however, and complained vociferously to the only other semblance of authority in the region—Lawrence Clarke, the Hudson's Bay Company's factor at Fort Carlton. Clarke, in turn, did his best to complain to those higher up about the affair, claiming that the Métis "were in open revolt against the authority of the Canadian government."

The statement was quite obviously false, and Clarke must have known it. At their first meeting in 1873, the Métis had explicitly acknowledged Canadian authority. Yet the oath did nothing to change the fact that no Canadian authority to speak of existed in the region, and that steps had to be taken to maintain order in the communities. Few could have guessed that doing so would be interpreted as recalcitrance to Canada. Indeed, these laws were simply the continuation of the long-standing unwritten code of the prairies that Clarke knew about and tacitly accepted for years. Clarke may well have harboured personal reasons for his actions—perhaps jealousy at the power exercised by Dumont in the region while he wielded so little, perhaps a dislike of the man Clarke saw behind the entire government, Father André. Otherwise, his unduly alarmist reactions can have little explanation.

A few exaggerated newspaper headlines later, government officials arrived with a small detachment of Mounties. They quickly realized that Clarke's reports had indeed been overblown and that the rules of the buffalo hunt were necessary on the still-wild frontier. However, in their discussions with the Métis, the council also decided, as a show of good faith, to return the fines it had imposed on the forerunners who had initiated the whole mess. It was a diplomatic and forgiving gesture, but it also spelled the end of their experimental government. With no power to impose its laws, the president and council naturally lost their sanction.

CHAPTER FOUR

Louis Riel Returns

We do not consider that we are asking too much.

WHEN THE MANITOBA FREE PRESS got wind of the incident involving the renegade buffalo hunters, the paper promptly began its fear mongering. Reported in its headlines: "Another Stand Against Canadian Government Authority in the North-West; a Provisional Government in Carlton; M. Louis Riel Again to the Front; 10,000 Crees on the Warpath; Fort Carlton in Possession of the Rebels; A Number of Mounted Police Killed." At the time it was speculative, sensationalist and wildly inaccurate journalism of the lowest order. Yet it is eerie how prophetic these headlines would eventually come to be less than 10 years later, excepting of course the numbers of Cree. And what happened in the intervening decade that would induce a peaceful people who had begun to organize a government explicitly loyal and subservient to the Canadian authorities to explode into open rebellion? Land.

The Saskatchewan Métis were never guaranteed any legal title to the land that had long been *de facto* theirs. As early as 1878, Gabriel Dumont had held meetings and organized for a petition to be drawn up and forwarded to the government, asking that the Saskatchewan Métis be granted legal title to the land they had settled. They believed this land, not without some justification, to be theirs by birthright and ancestry in a way similar to the land title recognized in the Native treaties.

The virtual extinction of the buffalo in 1880–81 coupled with the concurrent final collapse of the buffalo hunt underscored the importance, indeed the necessity, of farmland to call their own. Meanwhile, Métis and white settlements had increased in the region throughout the 1870s and into the 1880s. Many, including the white settlers, wondered anxiously what would become of the land upon which they were still legally viewed as mere squatters.

The Canadian government had made prior arrangements to set aside much of the land in the North-West for the Hudson's Bay Company and the Canadian Pacific Railway. Would this include land already settled? The matter of the square quarter sections that the Canadian government seemed remarkably stubborn in applying over the entire North-West was a further aggravation to the Métis, who had settled their lands in long, narrow riverfront strips, according to the custom of their forefathers. Would title to these properties be respected?

Despite repeated entreaties and petitions to government authorities, their questions remained unanswered. Over the years, the Canadian government received many third-party pleas that Métis claims to land title be respected, together with dire warnings of what might happen if justice was not forthcoming. What is more, these appeals often came from well-respected figures who either lived or had lived in the region and knew it well. But their entreaties and advice seemed to fall on deaf ears in Ottawa.

In 1882, Dumont was instrumental in sending yet another petition to Ottawa. It concluded: "Having been so long regarded as the masters of this country, having defended it against the Natives at the cost of our blood, we do not consider that we are asking too much when we call on the government to allow us to occupy our lands in peace and to exempt us from the regulations by making free grants of land to the Métis of the North-West." Silence and inaction met this appeal as well.

"There's one man who could do what I wanted to do, and that's Louis Riel."

The issue of land rights came to a head in 1884, when the Saskatchewan Métis decided that it was time to take action. Gabriel called a meeting on March 22, which was attended by about 30 prominent Métis. Dumont addressed the gathered assembly in Cree, speaking with a humourless gravity that instantly got everyone's attention. He began by telling the assembly that the meeting was to be kept secret and made all present take an oath to that effect. Only after everyone was sworn in did Dumont continue.

Dumont recounted the long list of Métis grievances and the reasons why they were just. Yet, in spite of the legitimacy of their claims and years of repeated protests and petitions, they had nothing to show for their efforts.

"And let me tell you, my friends," an obviously exasperated Dumont continued, "that's not the end of it. The government will never give us anything! They stole our land with promises, and now when they've got control, they're laughing at us. They don't intend to grant us the slightest thing in return for the soil where generations of our ancestors sleep. No. We'll never get anything from them, until we take matters into our own hands and force the government to give us justice."

Dumont took the time to retrace his work over the previous decades in trying to organize the Natives, encouraging them to present a united and solid front in the face of invasion by white settlers. He was also candid about his own limitations. He was quite aware that he was not educated well enough to inspire confidence in the local white population, who may have shared some of their concerns. He also knew that he wasn't the best choice to deal with the bureaucrats and politicians from the East.

"But before I sit down, I want to tell you that there's one man who could do what I wanted to do, and that's Louis Riel. Let's bring him back from Montana."

A collective gasp may have gone up from the assembly at the mention of Louis Riel, who was now living south of the border in Montana. But it didn't take long for the group to reach consensus: Louis Riel must return.

When the meeting concluded, the assembly members cautiously proceeded to broach the idea with the wider community. In April, several hundred Métis discussed Riel's return at a larger meeting in front of the senior Isidore Dumont's house and eventually agreed to ask Riel for his help. The Métis admirably continued in their efforts to unite the Natives, the white farmers and the Métis but did not stop here. At what proved to be a stormy meeting in May, the Métis persuaded the white farmers and English Half-breeds in the area to get on board with their plan to bring Riel back. Frustrations with Ottawa had reached such heights that they were able to achieve community consensus, and enough money was raised to send a delegation to Montana.

On May 19, Gabriel Dumont, Jimmie Isbister, Moise Ouellette and Michel Dumas headed south to meet with the legendary Métis spokesman, Louis Riel. They arrived at St. Peter's Mission on Sunday, June 4, while Riel was in church. Dumont asked an older woman if she would go into the

Louis Riel (1844–85), taken when he was living in Montana around 1883

chapel to inform Riel that he had visitors from far away. Riel emerged shortly from the humble house of worship, walking towards the party with no small measure of wariness in his step. Dumont could not contain himself and went forward to meet this man of whom he had heard so much.

"Hello, Monsieur Riel," Gabriel said, taking Riel's hand. "Me and my companion, we have travelled a long way to meet you."

Riel's unease was transparent to Dumont. The gruff buffalo hunter watched Louis' nervous eyes dart from himself to his retinue several paces behind him. An awkward silence persisted.

Finally, Louis Riel spoke. "Yes, I can see that you have travelled a great distance." Riel forced a smile. "But I'm afraid you have me at a disadvantage. For while you seem to know who I am, I can't say the same for you."

"Pardon me," Gabriel responded. "You do not know me, but I'm sure you know my name. I am Gabriel Dumont."

Riel's look changed from discomfort to surprise. He stared in awe at the massive buffalo hunter. The second time he spoke it took him even longer to find his tongue.

"Of course. I know your name well," Riel tried to chuckle, but only managed a nervous sort of snigger. It was obvious to Dumont that the former Métis leader did not receive visitors often. "Who hasn't heard your name?" Riel said.

"Well then, we're on common ground," Dumont responded, smiling generously, trying to put Riel at ease. "I know of you as well and have come to talk about matters north of the border."

The tension crept away from Louis' face. "Monsieur Dumont, of course I am interested in hearing what you have to say, but whatever it is, I'm sure the word of the Lord takes precedence. I hope you will let me finish Mass before we continue."

Riel directed the delegation to his home, where his wife Marguerite was tending to their children. So it was that within the hour, Dumont and his men were crowded around a small table in Louis' humble home, telling him about the problems in their community, asking the architect of the Red River resistance for his assistance. Try as he might, Louis Riel could not contain his pleasure at being so consulted. Gabriel spoke the delegation's last words.

"We need your help. Will you please come with us to Saskatchewan?"

Louis Riel gave his cryptic response. "God has helped me understand why you have made this long trip, and since there are four of you who have arrived on the fourth, and you wish to leave with a fifth, I cannot answer you today. You must wait until the fifth. I will give you my answer in the morning."

The following day, they received their answer as promised. "It has been 15 years since I gave my heart to my country," Riel began. "I am ready to give it again now, but I cannot leave my little family. If you can arrange for them to come, then I will go with you."

Dumont and the others answered that they would gladly make room in their carts for Riel's family. Riel spent a few days wrapping up his affairs in St. Peter's Mission, Montana, and then the small party, now slightly larger, began its return journey to the banks of the South Saskatchewan River.

Years later, Dumont recalled the reception Louis Riel received on his arrival: "The 22nd day after we left the mission, we arrived at Fish Creek, where 60 Métis had come to meet us." It was a boisterous, noisy welcome, the young men riding about, firing off a *feu de joie* from their hunting rifles and shouting out Riel's name. As the party moved on to the Tourond farm, just above the creek, the welcome party grew much larger. Fifty cartloads of Métis had come out to meet the hero of the Red River resistance, the man upon whom they pinned so many of their hopes. Women and children were there, but also some of the older patriarchs of the bygone buffalo hunt, who wanted to lay eyes upon this man and greet him. The large procession made its way to Gabriel's Crossing, where Madeleine welcomed Marguerite Riel and her family into the Dumont home. The cheer and exultation in the air was infectious, and everyone, including Gabriel Dumont, wore a wide grin when Mrs. Riel met Mrs. Dumont. That night, a sea of tents surrounded Gabriel's Crossing.

After he settled in, Riel continued the Métis strategy of presenting Ottawa with as broad and united a front of Western grievances as possible. This approach, many of the inhabitants felt, would force Ottawa to finally take action. He threw himself into negotiations and coalition building with the local people—white and Métis, English and French—and in the succeeding months a grand, and dearly hoped final, list of Western demands began to emerge.

It was here that Dumont's influence came into play. After Riel arrived, Gabriel slipped into the background. This sort of political dealing and petition drafting was not really the veteran hunter's talent. He was happy to let Riel do the politicking. However, with attempts to build a broader coalition, the issue of whether to include Native grievances in the petition arose.

Dumont was strongly in favour. He had observed the dire situation of the Natives in the North-West over the past few years. Times had been hard indeed, as the great beasts upon which these cultures had depended for centuries vanished from the vast, open spaces they had always known. Although the government had promised the Natives assistance in making the transition to a more sedentary lifestyle, the rounds of treaties signed in the late 1870s proved to be so many well-packaged lies. Many Native tribes lived in abject poverty and in a state of near starvation.

This state of affairs pained Dumont. He had spent the past two and more decades of his life building and improving relations between the Métis and the Native tribes of the Plains. Dumont, his father and his brother had even travelled to meet with their traditional enemies, the Sioux, in their own territory. They concluded a successful treaty with the Dakota Sioux that, over time, substantially improved relations. These negotiations were difficult and often dangerous, yet Dumont continued to broker peaceful relations. His tireless efforts at coalition building eventually bound the Saskatchewan Métis in loose alliances with

Gabriel Dumont, taken in the 1880s, in fur and waistcoat

all the tribes, from the warlike Sioux to the fiercely independent Blackfoot Confederacy. Although he engaged in these negotiations for humanist reasons, he had another motivation as well. Dumont was aware of a connection to these original peoples that went deeper even than blood. They were all a part of the culture of the buffalo, the culture of the old Plains that was now being transformed by forces from the East.

"They are our kin," Gabriel told one visitor to the St. Laurent region in September 1884, "and when they starve, they come to us for help. We have to feed them." The treaty obligations that Dumont had made with the Natives simply had to be fulfilled as a point of honour. Yet the government, which also signed treaties, did not adhere to the spirit, or often even the letter of their agreements.

"The government does not treat the Indians properly," Gabriel said on the same occasion.

Dumont and others among the Métis did their best to give the Natives what food they could, but the times were also difficult for their own people, and they rightly felt as if they were struggling to fulfil a responsibility that should not have been theirs.

At length, Dumont persuaded Riel to include the grievances of the Natives in the grand petition he was composing. It was a difficult decision politically, because the choice cost the movement some of the more lukewarm support they had enjoyed from the white settlers in nearby Prince Albert and Battleford. With a changed focus, work on the petition continued throughout the fall, and it was finally sent off to Ottawa in December. The petition made demands in four basic areas. It pressed for greater democracy—an elected provincial government and better representation of the area in Ottawa. It sought to resolve the long and deeply frustrating issue of land through modifications to the Dominion Lands Act, by the issuing of scrip and land patents to the still officially "squatting" Métis. It called for the federal government to live up to its treaty obligations with the Native tribes. And lastly, in a concession to the white settlers, the petition asked for a reduction in railway tariffs and the promise of an extension of the Canadian Pacific Railway north to the Hudson Bay.

For weeks the Métis waited but no response came from the Macdonald government. Frustrations mounted again amid wild speculation and alternating waves of pessimism and optimism. In early February, Ottawa's response finally trickled its way down to the Métis gathered in and around Batoche, and it proved to be the crucial turning point along the thorny path to a rebellion that no one wanted. Even though the prime minister continued to receive warnings about the state of affairs in the area, John A. Macdonald still did not seem to think the situation needed serious, prompt attention and action. Instead, Macdonald made a vague promise to set up a commission to examine Métis grievances later in the year.

The Métis had heard such empty words before, but this time words would not suffice. Far from it, the Métis were outraged. Riel, upon hearing the news, was beside himself with anger.

He yelled his response at a room full of prominent Métis: "In 40 days, Ottawa will have my answer!"

Dumont's reaction was more subdued. "All the work of the past few months," he said to Riel calmly, "all this negotiation, petitions, talk...it's all been a waste. Ottawa doesn't understand us."

Angry meetings and discussions tumbled quickly upon the heels of the Macdonald government's response to the Métis petition, and the possibility of armed resistance to the Canadian government bubbled out into the open. On March 5, a group of leading Métis, including Dumont and Riel took an oath to "save our country from wicked government by taking up arms if necessary." As later actions proved, in taking up arms, these people still earnestly hoped to avoid bloodshed. They did, however, increasingly think that a show of force—the seizing of property and prisoners—was necessary to get Ottawa's attention. Not all Métis favoured the aggressive new stance. One of the dissenters was Charles Nolin, a former Red River Métis who objected to Riel's leadership in 1869, and who was Riel's cousin. Nolin refused to take the March 5 oath, instead urging that the Métis hold a novena—a period of prayers and devotion lasting nine consecutive days. The Métis leadership acceded to the proposal, and the novena was scheduled to begin on March 10.

It was during the novena that the long-brewing split between the local Roman Catholic clergy and the Métis movement became irrevocable. Throughout the events leading up to that fateful March, the priests had stood aloof from the proceedings, a distance and indecision that long concerned the parishioners of their flock. Indeed, Dumont had fairly begged a group of priests gathered at Batoche under Bishop Grandin for their guidance the previous September. But the priests remained conspicuously silent.

On Sunday, March 15, six days into the novena, the Métis crowded into the church at St. Laurent to hear Father Fourmond say Mass. Thinking he might take some of the wind out of rebellious sails, Fourmond sermonized on the sin of resistance to authority and even threatened to withhold the sacraments from any Métis who took up arms in defiance of the government. In delivering the grave threat to the pious Métis, Fourmond had seriously misjudged the situation. It turned out that he was actually pouring fuel on the fire that was simmering in the hearts of his congregation.

Riel stood up in the church and openly defied Father Fourmond. "What is this?" Louis leapt to his feet, interrupting the sermon. "Is the Church now preaching the words of Ottawa? If it is, Father, let me warn you that the words that come from that city cannot be counted on."

"Louis Riel!" came Fourmond's roaring response. "How dare you interrupt God's service!"

"This is not God's service," Louis replied. "It is the prime minister's."

With these words, the devoutly religious Louis Riel turned and walked out of the church, followed closely by the rest of the congregation. The Métis would not have the church's support in the upcoming conflict. Father André had long since openly opposed Riel and even acted as the intermediary for the Macdonald government to deliver a bribe to Riel, if only he would agree to return to Montana. Riel refused, but the encounter was probably yet another piece of evidence that led Riel to some extreme conclusions about the need to reform his faith—and his place in such a reformation.

Nevertheless, the Métis still hoped for peace, although preparation for war now began in earnest. During the novena, Dumont travelled throughout the surrounding Métis communities, gathering and gauging support. He also visited the nearby Native tribes at Chief Beardy's and One Arrow's reserves. Everywhere rifles were being readied, just like the Métis used to do in preparation for their great hunts, and frightened informants were reporting to the local authorities.

Yet even with tempers boiling over at the 11th hour, the situation might have been saved. After all, a single shot had yet to be fired in anger. Had the federal authorities in Ottawa responded to the alarming news of growing unrest in the North-West with a concrete plan to address the Métis grievances, things might have turned out differently. What the situation called for was a strong shove in the direction of peace. What occurred was a nudge in the opposite direction.

On March 17, Lawrence Clarke, factor of the HBC post, ran into a group of Métis at Batoche's ferry. Clarke addressed the men with foolhardy condescension.

"Have you received any answer from Ottawa about your lands?"

Napoleon Nault, one of the leading members of the group, said that they had not.

"I didn't think so," Clarke scoffed. "In fact, I'm sure that the only answer you're going to get will be bullets."

The men were suddenly all ears. "What do you mean by that?" Nault snapped.

"It won't be long now," Clarke replied. "There are nearly 100 soldiers coming. I saw them at Humboldt, and tomorrow or the next day, Riel and Dumont will be taken."

Clarke was lying. He hadn't seen any such force, but he made up the story to frighten the Métis into submission. Instead of frightening the Métis, however, Clarke only incited them. The prospect that the authorities might come to arrest Riel and Dumont was intolerable to the Métis, and it galvanized their support for the more drastic measures that would soon follow.

CHAPTER FIVE

Insurrection

*"This, it seems, is the only language
Ottawa understands."*

AS FAR AS DUMONT WAS CONCERNED, the rebellion had begun.
On March 18, 1885, the day after the run-in with Lawrence
Clarke, a crowd of angry Métis met outside the church of St.
Antoine de Padoue on the outskirts of Batoche. A priest
named Julien Moulin stood atop the church's main stairs,
calling on the men to disperse, but his voice was lost in the
angry din.

When Riel and Dumont arrived in mid-afternoon, a great
cheer erupted from the gathered men. Parting the crowd, the
two leaders walked up the steps to where Father Moulin was
still standing.

"It is important that we have a meeting immediately,
Father," Louis said. "We need to use the church."

"The house of God will not be sullied by your politics,"
Moulin replied.

That was when Louis decided he'd had enough of the Saskatchewan clergy.

"Get out of my way!" he yelled at Moulin, grabbing the priest by the shoulder. "Rome has fallen!" Riel tossed Moulin into the crowd. "Take him!" he shouted to the men below. "I never want to see the face of this pretender again!"

Once they were settled inside, Dumont was the first to speak, his rumbling voice spilling over the pews, silencing the buzz of armed men's conversation like a judge's gavel.

"We are told that the police are coming to take Louis Riel. They call him a criminal. His crime? Standing up for our people." Gabriel walked across the front of the church and put his hand on Louis' shoulder. "Just as he worked for Red River against Ottawa so many years ago, so too has he worked tirelessly for us. But this time we cannot let him run into exile. This time we must make a stand for him."

The men sounded their agreement in unison, filling the church with their shouts. Riel stepped forward to give his response, and the crowd in the church instantly went quiet.

"Gabriel, I thank you, as I thank all of you," Riel said, his voice choking with emotion. "I know how this works. I've been here before. We send petitions; they send soldiers to take us—Gabriel and me. In their eyes, it is I who have done wrong. The government hates me because I already made them give in once. This time they will give up nothing." Louis paused there, his eyes going from the gathered men to where Dumont was standing.

"I say to you now," Louis continued, "that I think it would be better for me to go. I must leave you, and I feel I should go now. Once I am gone you may be able to get what you want more easily." A few men in the pews began shouting their objections, but Louis kept speaking over them. "Yes, I really think it would be better if I went back to Montana."

That was when the whole crowd offered their resounding rejection to Louis' idea. The church became a cacophony of disagreement. Gabriel Dumont stepped forward again.

"All in favour of taking up arms, raise your hands."

Every man in the church rose in unison, holding rifles and revolvers aloft. Gabriel had his army.

The next day, the Saskatchewan Métis, led by Louis Riel, elected a provisional government, which then chose Gabriel Dumont as adjutant general by acclamation and a governing council. Louis Riel refused any formal position in the government, arguing that the regime should be made up of the people who were rebelling—Gabriel's Métis. Still, Riel exercised tremendous authority over the provisional government. Taking on the role of prophet rather than president, he lent the governing body a biblical weight, christening the council the Exovedate, its members Exovedes—Latin for "out of the flock." Thus Riel, the prophet, enjoyed more power over his flock than any president could ever have over a governing council.

Dumont promptly set up his military headquarters at the home of a Métis named Norbert Delorme. It was shortly after the meeting at St. Antoine that Gabriel announced his intentions to a group of armed men.

"We are now in open revolt," he said. "From now on, when I see a government man I will take him prisoner. I will not ask any questions. I will not say much at all, but let the barrel of my gun do all the talking." The bristly Métis hunter looked at the assembled men before continuing. "You may think I am going too far, but no." Gabriel tapped the stock of his rifle that was slung over his shoulder. "This, it seems, is the only language Ottawa understands."

Indeed, the wheels of insurrection had begun to grind, as local Métis and Natives began flocking to St. Laurent parish, bringing with them Winchesters, old muskets and bows and arrows.

Members of the Saskatchewan Métis provisional government from left to right: Ignace Poitras, Pierre Parenteau, Baptiste Parenteau, Pierre Gariepy, Ignace Poitras, Jr., Alberta Monkman, Pierre Vandal, Baptiste Vandal, Joseph Arcand, Maxime Dubois, James Short, Pierre Henry, Baptiste Tourond, Emmanuel Champagne, Kit-a-wa-how (Alex Cagen, ex-chief of the Muskeg Lake Indians). The accuracy of these names has not been verified because there are more people in the photo than names given. It is assumed, however, that the names provided are only of the men whose faces are visible and recognizable.

After the rebellion many of the leaders fled to Montana to avoid prosecution by the Canadian government. But these councillors surrendered or were captured after the Battle for Batoche in April 1885 and are shown here in front of the courthouse in Regina at the time of their trial. Many were tried on the charge of treason-felony, a lesser offence than the charge of high treason, which was levelled against Riel. Most of the councillors pleaded guilty, and the sentences they received ranged from conditional discharge to seven years in prison. When the general amnesty for the rebels was announced by the Canadian government, all of the rebels in prison were released early.

One of Gabriel's first acts as adjutant general was the organization of his warriors according to the structure of the buffalo hunt. He chose two principal lieutenants, Joseph Delorme and Patrice Tourond. He then grouped his 300 warriors into two scouting companies, chosen from the best of the Métis horsemen, and 10 fighting companies. He then appointed captains to lead each company.

Dumont shortly demonstrated his resolve. With a company of armed men, he rode to George Kerr's store, intending to appropriate the arms and ammunition there. As luck would have it, John Lash, the Indian agent at One Arrow's reserve, and his interpreter, William Tompkins, happened to be in the store buying a sack of potatoes. Dumont took advantage of the opportunity.

"I am taking you prisoner," he informed Lash bluntly.

A surprised Lash was at a loss for words. "Oh? Why?"

"We have taken up arms against the government," Dumont responded. "We intend to take prisoner all those who work for the government."

The Indian agent dared not question the well-armed Dumont any further, but peacefully surrendered.

In taking prisoners, Dumont was abiding by the long-standing Plains tradition of taking and holding hostages to be used in negotiations. Dumont was so assured in taking action that he only later thought to inform Riel. Louis approved, quick to acknowledge the advantage of hostages in potential discussions with the Canadian government. The incident raises the question, however, about which of the two men was truly in command of the Métis at this point. Indeed, George Kerr, who witnessed Louis and Gabriel in discussion shortly after the capture of Lash, noted that Dumont was definitely in charge.

Others observers agreed, noting that, although Riel seemed to exercise an overarching influence, the Métis warriors took their orders directly from Dumont. It makes sense that Louis would take a back seat to Dumont when the time for action was upon them. Dumont was the hunter-warrior, quite at ease in this world of decisive action and fateful consequence. Riel, on the other hand, was more of an abstract thinker—a visionary who turned pale and hesitated when his beautiful plans confronted a much uglier reality.

Dumont next rode to the only other non-Métis store in the immediate vicinity, that of Henry Walters. There, over the angry objections of the proprietor, he appropriated more arms, ammunition and provisions and captured more prisoners. Dumont also sent out parties to cut the telegraph lines to the north and south of Batoche. The telegraph company sent two men to repair the severed lines, but a Métis patrol led by Gabriel's brother Isidore and Augustin Laframboise promptly captured them. In an incident quite revealing of the still-peaceful nature of most Métis, Dumont asked his returning men if they had bothered to disarm their prisoners. When they answered that they had not, Dumont was not alarmed.

Hillyard Mitchell, an esteemed merchant from Duck Lake, and an English Half-breed named Thomas McKay came to meet with the Métis leadership, hoping to calm things in Batoche. McKay managed to offend Dumont almost immediately. When Riel greeted him with an extended hand, McKay dismissed the revered Métis leader and walked straight up to Dumont, addressing him with barely concealed disdain.

"Gabriel, you have led your people ably for many years, but you cannot possibly understand what is happening around you now. I must warn you; this revolt is a mistake."

Dumont's look was dangerous. He was a physical man, more accustomed to action, but he forced himself to respond with words.

"Tom, it is *you* who are making the mistake. I am not being controlled by men who are hundreds of miles away, men who cannot possibly know what it is to live the way we do. I am not a slave to the Hudson's Bay Company. Although you are Métis and have the same rights to gain as we do, you have gone against us. You come here acting as though you speak wisdom, but I doubt whether you have even a spoonful of good sense."

McKay began to respond when Gabriel, at the end of his patience, silenced him.

"Don't say another word, Tom. Your blood is all water; your words are poison. If not for the years between us, I would have taken you prisoner by now."

Tom still tried reasoning with the Métis leader. "Gabriel—"

"Not another word," Gabriel said. "Now get out of my sight before I do something rash."

Riel, Dumont and the Métis council chose to send two messengers of their own, Max Lépine and Charles Nolin, to Fort Carlton with Mitchell and McKay. On March 22, they took their ultimatum to Fort Carlton's North-West Mounted Police Superintendent, Lief Crozier, demanding that he surrender the fort and the town of Battleford, together with all government properties in his jurisdiction. In return, they offered to let Crozier's men go unmolested, as long as they did nothing to disturb the peace. The Métis even offered to furnish those who wished to leave the area with teams of horses and provisions enough to reach Qu'Appelle.

"But in case of non-acceptance," the ultimatum concluded in harsh terms, "we intend to attack you, when tomorrow, the Lord's Day is over; and to commence without delay a war of extermination upon all those who have shown themselves hostile to our rights."

Crozier took the threats seriously. Not only was he gravely outnumbered, but Fort Carlton and Battleford were notoriously indefensible. Fort Carlton, in particular, had been constructed with economic considerations; its layout was especially vulnerable to attack. To the south and east, steep, wooded hills offered a clear view of the compound behind the wooden palisades.

Leif Crozier (1847–1901), NWMP Superintendent of Fort Carlton in 1880, five years before the battle at Duck Lake

As one of the volunteers at the fort glumly surmised, "Those hills offer a beautiful spot for sharpshooters to pot us as we walk about."

Moreover, the only practical evacuation route, from the fort—a single cart trail heading north through thick woods—almost begged to be used for an ambush. So poor was the location that the veterans under Crozier's command conceded that about 20 well-positioned snipers could effectively lay siege to the entire

fort. Battleford, with almost no defenders and incomplete forti-
fications, was in even worse shape. However, with no shots yet
fired, and the swaggering presence of volunteer soldiers from
Prince Albert at the fort, Superintendent Crozier, although
undoubtedly alarmed, refused to submit to the Métis threat.

On March 24, word reached Batoche that the Mounted
Police were using Duck Lake as a reconnaissance base. Riel
and Dumont met with the Exovedate to decide on a response
to the threat. Gabriel pushed for action. In the days previous,
the Métis general's frustration had been steadily building. The
date given to Crozier in the Métis ultimatum had come and
gone, and the Métis forces had done nothing. Riel was still
hesitating. Time was slipping through their fingers, and with
it, Gabriel knew, whatever leverage the Métis had. Dumont
realized that the Métis held the advantage, while they were in
possession of the largest, most mobile and most effective
fighting force in the region. But it was only a matter of time
before Canadian forces began arriving from the East. Already,
one day earlier, Prime Minister Macdonald ordered General
Frederick D. Middleton to form a militia and head to the
Saskatchewan country. What the Métis lacked, under Riel's
moody leadership, was the initiative to act and use its force
to the fullest. Holding out the hope that Ottawa would send
diplomatic negotiators and trying to avoid violence, Louis
ordered Dumont and his warriors to stand down.

"But Louis," Dumont pleaded, "they have many more men,
arms and ammunition than we do. We will never win on the
open battlefield. We have to fight them in the darkness, raid
their supplies, strike terror into their hearts."

"Never," came Louis' stern rebuke. "We will not fight like
the savages they believe us to be. If we were fighting a war of
extermination, we could put every farm from here to Regina
to the torch and bring the sword upon women and children.

Major-General Frederick Middleton (1825–98), commanding officer of the force sent to put down the North-West Rebellion

But no, we are God's soldiers and will only strike when we are set upon. This is my word. This is the will of God."

It says much of Louis' influence over Gabriel that the hard-headed Métis warrior, girded for battle and convinced his guerrilla tactics would win the day, took Riel's preaching to heart and kept his equally eager Métis fighters from attacking. Indeed, Louis had come to occupy a lofty position among the Métis—if he wasn't quite a saint, he was almost there. Louis did nothing to discourage such musings. His system of government actively encouraged it.

Riel preached that Métis success depended on their purity and obedience to the Lord's word. The Exovedate and the issues it debated revealed the extent to which Riel had slipped into his convoluted spiritual vision. While the governing council presided over the minutiae of daily life—dispensing free passes for local ferries and even judging the ownership of stray cows—its primary focus was to remake the world from the ground up.

As Gabriel Dumont and his soldiers were plotting ways to repel the imminent Canadian attack, Riel's Exovedate was busy tackling abstract religious questions. Seizing the opportunity to enact the tenets of his lifelong theology that found its provenance in exile and insanity, Riel first declared that the Catholic Sabbath would be changed from Sunday to Saturday. He then had an old confidant of his, Bishop Bourget, formally recognized as the first "Pope of the New World." The council of Exovedes took the final step when it passed a resolution recognizing "Louis David Riel as a prophet in the service of Jesus Christ and Son of God and only Redeemer of the World."

Yet, even as Riel enshrined himself as a Métis holy man, Dumont pressed for action. Duck Lake lay a mere six miles from Batoche and approximately one-third of the way from Batoche to Fort Carlton. The small village commanded trails leading both to the fort and to the larger commercial centre of Prince Albert. Hillyard Mitchell's store, with its supply of provisions, was located there as well. Moreover, the population was split between Métis settlers and white merchants who were indecisive about their allegiances. Yet, despite all these facts, command of Duck Lake still hung in the air.

"You have given them all the advantages," Dumont confronted Riel in front of the debating council. "It has come to the point that they are riding freely right under our noses." Gabriel turned to the assembled men. "I tell you, we must ride out to Duck Lake, occupy it and take the supplies out of Mitchell's store."

A hesitant hum of agreement spread throughout the Exovedate. The councillors looked from Gabriel, even now armed and ready for action, to Louis Riel, whose brow was furrowed in concentration.

"We have taken up arms, and yet we just sit here," Gabriel continued. "But it isn't too late, if we move now, we could still take them by surprise."

"But it won't be easy," Riel objected. "They won't just let us get away with it."

Dumont's response was confident. "Give me 10 men, and put me in charge."

"Surely, we can spare 10 men," someone in the council said.

"So be it," Louis nodded. "Take your men, Gabriel, and may God go with you."

Dumont had heard a rumour that Mitchell planned to defend his store with a pitchfork if need be, but it turned out that, when confronted by the reality of the approaching Métis, Mitchell was somewhat wiser. Having received word that Dumont was on his way, Mitchell locked his store and fled. When Gabriel rode down on Duck Lake with his 10 hunters, the only man he found around the store was Magnus Burstein, an English Half-breed who worked as a clerk for Mitchell.

"Where's Mitchell?" Dumont demanded of the shopkeeper's assistant. "And where's the key?"

Burstein had no desire to help Dumont loot his employer's store and put on a hard, silent shell. Gabriel couldn't get anything out of him. The Métis leader quickly lost patience.

"Fine, fine," Gabriel said. "We'll break down the doors then."

Dumont moved to do just that when Burstein held up his hand. Deciding he had nothing to gain from watching Dumont tear his boss' store apart, Burstein came up with the key.

"I'll open the door for you, Gabriel. But I should tell you that you're wasting your time. Mitchell has already emptied it of anything valuable."

A disappointed Dumont soon discovered that Burstein was telling the truth. All of the guns had been removed, but they did find some lead shot scattered in the latrine ditch behind the store. Dumont made sure that his men made off with all the tobacco, buffalo robes and pemmican in the store. But the all-important arms that Dumont's ill-equipped forces so dearly needed were missing.

Dumont was hardly the timid type, and because Riel had given permission for his general to lead a force to Duck Lake, Dumont decided to press on. He led his small force to reconnoitre the trail leading to Fort Carlton. On the way, Dumont stopped to have tea with Chief Beardy and his people at their reserve. Although Chief Beardy remained officially neutral, he could not restrain some of the younger Cree braves from throwing themselves into the Métis rebellion, nor did he try.

"If you try to escape, I will kill you!"

Superintendent Crozier, worried by rumours that the Métis were moving his way, sent two men to observe Métis activity around Duck Lake on the evening of March 25. Harold Ross, the deputy sheriff from Prince Albert, and a surveyor named John Astley left the relative comfort and safety of Fort Carlton at about 10 PM. By midnight, Métis scouts reported the approach of the two men. Dumont took his brother Edouard and three others before galloping off into the moonlit night to meet the intruders. Still, Dumont showed laudable restraint.

"If they try to defend themselves, kill them," Dumont ordered his horsemen as they rode out. "If not, we will not harm them."

As the four neared the place on the far side of the lake where the two men had been spotted, Dumont grew more cautious.

He moved his small party off the trodden path through the snow, until they were behind a small bluff a few yards to the side of the trail. The men spoke in whispers, knowing their prey was close. Suddenly, Dumont caught sight of the two men silhouetted in the pale light. When they drew close enough, Dumont bellowed his commands to his riders.

"Go! Turn your horses loose! Get them!"

The Métis swooped down upon the surprised pair so swiftly that a surprised Sheriff Ross barely had time to cry, "They are upon us!" before being surrounded. The charge evidently shook the two so badly that Ross later claimed that they were set upon by a force of "between 60 and 100 men."

Dumont, leading the way, came up on the left side of Ross as the two frightened men had their horses in mid-turn.

"Stop!" Dumont thundered. "If you try to escape, I will kill you!"

"Why?" the panicked Ross said. "I am just a surveyor!"

Dumont was incredulous. "What are you trying to tell me? There is nothing to survey out here at this time of night."

The Métis general had heard enough. He swung his leg over the top of his horse with cat-like speed, grabbed Ross by the arms and yanked him out of his saddle. While Dumont was dealing with Ross, Astley nearly escaped. The other scout turned and urged his mount forward on the narrow trail. Behind him, Dumont, Ross and their two horses blocked pursuit. To either side of the path lay deep snow topped with a hard crust that would make for slow going. One of the Métis behind Dumont, Baptiste Deschamps, pulled his revolver, cocked the hammer and aimed at the retreating figure.

"Stop, or I'll shoot you!" Deschamps bellowed.

Startled, Astley turned in his saddle to see if the Métis really was taking aim, and the movement of his hands steered his mount into the deep snow off the trail. His horse stumbled and threw the startled rider. The Métis quickly collected him from the snow and brought him before Dumont, who had already disarmed and subdued Ross. Only after he stripped Astley of his weapons, did he speak.

"You are my prisoners, and I am taking you to Duck Lake. If you behave well, you will be well treated, but your horses are no longer yours."

The two were hardly in a position to argue. Dumont appropriated his prisoners' steeds and offered them his two worst horses for the ride back, which the two men indignantly refused.

On returning to Duck Lake, Dumont heard that one of his earlier prisoners had been asking for Sheriff Ross.

"He isn't sheriff tonight," Dumont answered, a crooked smile on his face.

The gathered men shared a laugh, dispelling some of the tension of the eventful night. In the meantime, Riel and his Métis council arrived at Duck Lake. Thinking that Gabriel and his riders had dealt with the Duck Lake spies, the Métis were about to return to Batoche. That was when Ross and Astley spoke. Perhaps believing they could gain some advantage by threatening the Métis, the new prisoners told them that Crozier had ordered a gang of men to ride into town to occupy Mitchell's store. Dumont took the warning seriously and leapt back on his horse, his trusted *Le Petit* at his side, and rode out with a few of his men to scout the trail to Fort Carlton for the remainder of the night.

"Now is the time, Crozier, to show if you have any sand in you."

Crozier actually had sent a party to take possession of the supplies at Mitchell's store, just as the prisoners had said. Eighteen North-West Mounted Police and volunteers, four scouts and eight sleighs left Fort Carlton in the early morning of March 26, led by police sergeant Alfred Stewart. Thomas McKay accompanied the party as it headed out of the fort into the bitingly cold air of the still-black morning towards Duck Lake. They arrived at Duck Lake just as the first traces of light coloured the sky.

Dumont, having maintained a steady patrol throughout the night, had just returned to Duck Lake for a well-deserved breakfast when the sentries sounded the alert. The men scrambled back onto their horses, and in a tumult, galloped back across Duck Lake towards Fort Carlton. Dumont found himself behind his three men and, not liking the unfamiliar rear position, gambled on catching up to them by heading off the track. Instead of gaining on them, Dumont got caught in the deeper snow and lost even more time. At one point, the distressed general estimated that he trailed his men by roughly a quarter of a mile.

Shortly after crossing the lake, the three ran into the scouts of the police detachment, including Thomas McKay. The Half-breed McKay wisely ordered the other scouts to turn about to warn the main body of the column that Dumont was approaching, and a feverish pursuit followed. Seeing his scouts thundering back towards him, Sergeant Stewart drew his sleighs into a rough, defensive semi-circle and waited.

They didn't have to wait long. The three pursuing Métis kept coming until they were dangerously close but then pulled their horses to a halt. They sat on their pawing mounts, unsure of what to do next. An alarmed Dumont, still behind them but approaching fast, sized up the situation and called to his men.

"What are you doing? Why are you still on your horses? Can't you see they might shoot! Get off your horses and get ready to defend yourselves!" They did as he said.

Dumont caught up with his men. In one fluid motion, he grabbed his carbine and slid off his mount, giving it a firm slap on the neck to send it away from the danger. The grizzled Métis warrior crept towards the police column like a stout mountain lion, scoping out the dark forms of the enemy and intent on seizing the initiative. He stared at their weapons lustfully, thinking how valuable their arms and ammunitions would be to his under-supplied army. At the very least, Dumont intended to push the police and see how they would respond.

When the Métis commander, with his men close behind him, came to within 25 yards of the sleighs, one of the police sergeants yelled out, "Stop right there, or I'll shoot!"

"Don't try it," the unruffled Dumont snarled back, still advancing while taking aim at the sergeant. "I'll shoot you first."

The sergeant took another look at Dumont and decided to lay his rifle across his knees. By this time, Dumont was a mere 10 to 15 yards away, and he brashly decided to charge the distance. In two or three leaps, he was upon the surprised sergeant. Dumont fed him the butt of his carbine, sending the officer tumbling back into his sleigh, dazed and bleeding heavily. As the Mountie fell backwards, his rifle went off, shattering the stillness of the March morning.

A moment later, every man on each side had his gun drawn, aimed and cocked. One frayed nerve could have ignited a terrible slaughter, but no one acted, and the Mexican standoff stretched on over a handful of seconds. The sergeant, still dazed, scrambled clumsily back to his feet and groped for the revolver at his belt. Dumont, who was standing right there, pulled his revolver and trained it on the wounded man.

"Move, and you die," he said evenly to the sergeant. Gabriel was not the type to lose a game of chicken.

It was then that the Canadians realized that they were just as awed by the defiant hunter as they were afraid. Every one of them knew of Dumont's legendary reputation. So too did the sergeant. He stopped reaching for his gun and slowly raised both hands into the air. McKay rushed in to intervene.

"Look out, Gabriel," he challenged Dumont to his face, "if you don't back down, it'll be the end of you!"

"Look out yourself," Dumont replied, unable to comprehend how McKay could side against his own people. "I'll make sure that if any man gets it tonight, it'll be you." He sized up the English Half-breed with transparent disdain. "Don't you realize that there are Métis fighting to the death with us?"

McKay began to answer, but hearing his voice sent a spasm of rage up Gabriel's back. Suddenly fed up with the man he consided a traitor, Gabriel lifted his rifle to take a swing at him while keeping the pistol in his other hand steady on the sergeant. McKay tried to turn his horse, putting the animal's hind legs off the path on the high side and into the deep snow. McKay was now closer to the ground, giving Dumont an even more tempting target. He swung with such force that McKay would have certainly been knocked from his saddle, but luckily for him, his horse made one quick movement, pulling its rider back up. The butt end of *Le Petit* only grazed McKay's back as he spurred his horse and shot forward, away from the angry arc of Dumont's second swing.

Gabriel looked around to find another officer in a different sleigh taking direct aim at him. Calmly, Dumont trained his rifle on the man, whose sudden onset of uncertainty was all too obvious, even in the half-light of early morning. Still, both sides were locked in a deadly standoff. Again, McKay was the one who broke it, calling for the detachment to begin a retreat. One by one, the men complied, slowly backing away from the scene, keeping their weapons aimed at their foes. In another moment, they dashed headlong away from Dumont and his small group of hunters.

Gabriel's men, flushed with the excitement of watching their leader stare down an entire troop of police, wanted to pursue the column, but Gabriel restrained them. The Métis general knew that his four men were not enough to stop the plus-20 force from leaving. And throughout the standoff, Louis Riel's directive of non-violence ran through his mind, stopping him from being the one to fire the first shot. Nevertheless, Dumont could not resist the temptation to taunt McKay for his flight.

"What did you come here for, blockhead?" he called after the Half-breed. "We were told that you would come with men. Where are they?" The laughter of the Métis travelled far over the snow-choked plain.

Although the encounter was not quite the incredible coup that Dumont had hoped for, the Métis still returned to Duck Lake in triumph. Four of them had won a contest of guts and will against a far superior force. Dumont, in particular, certainly added to the lustre of his reputation. There wasn't a hunter among them who doubted their general's bravery, skill or determination. Again, though, the returning Métis scarcely had time to sit down, eat and receive the congratulations of their compatriots before the cry of the sentries went up again: "The police are coming!"

Well in advance of the repulsed column's return to Fort Carlton, a courier brought back word of the unexpected reversal, and the humiliating news stirred the entire fort. Superintendent Crozier was reluctant to respond immediately, however, and for good reason. He knew that his superior, Commissioner Irvine was marching in from Prince Albert with a force of more than 100 men to reinforce him, and that these men were expected to arrive at any time. Crozier, a trained officer, knew full well that any action taken before the arrival of these troops would be foolish. He also knew that Dumont possessed a force superior to his, both in numbers and in potential fighting ability on terrain that the Métis knew so well. His reason was instructing him to sit tight.

Dissident voices, however, were telling him otherwise. The Hudson's Bay Company factor, Lawrence Clarke, took a swipe at the officer's pride. Taking it on himself to inform Crozier of the mood in the fort, Clarke gave reports of unrest, impatience and anger among the men. The Prince Albert volunteers under his command, more so than the Mounties, were especially eager for a fight and grumbled about all the sitting around.

"Are we to be turned back by a parcel of Half-breeds?" Clarke asked Crozier, shocked that the superintendent had to even think about it. "Now is the time, Crozier, to show if you have any sand in you."

Superintendent Crozier was still reluctant, but after Clarke and the citizen volunteers from Prince Albert began to whisper that he was a coward, Crozier was goaded into action. He quickly marshalled his forces and set out to join with Sergeant Stewart's returning column. The combined total of 56 North-West Mounted Police, 43 volunteers and teamsters and a venerable 7-pound cannon left for Duck Lake at around 10 AM on the morning of March 26, 1885, determined this time not to be turned back by a mere "parcel of Half-breeds."

"Where are you going with all those guns, grandson?"

Learning from his scouts that a substantially larger force now moved on Duck Lake, Dumont galloped back across the lake, accompanied by about 25 men, with more joining in from the village as quickly as they could ready themselves. A column of Métis hunters rode up from Batoche with Louis Riel at the head of the column holding an enormous bronze crucifix. His arrival brought Gabriel's force to over 200 Métis and Natives. As they thundered towards their foe, Dumont turned to his brother Isidore and the others around them.

"I don't want to start killing them, I want to take prisoners," he stressed, reminding his men of the strict policy of not firing the first shot that had been decided upon by himself, Riel and the entire Métis council. Gabriel's faith in Louis' leadership was firm enough that he still thought that they could avoid violence.

"Only if they start firing on us," Dumont finished, "do we fire back."

Volunteer Alex Stewart was among Crozier's forward scouts, and as he approached Duck Lake, he saw the Métis and their Native brethren—their bodies painted in the garish colours of war. They charged over the rise towards him, whooping as they came. Stewart wheeled his horse, shouting out to the main body of Crozier's forces.

"Enemy here!"

Then he feverishly galloped back towards more friendly ranks, while Dumont and his men prepared their line of battle.

Hearing the warning, Crozier halted right where he was, halfway up a long, gentle incline, and quickly swung his column around into a semicircle stretching across the path to Duck Lake. His men tipped their sleighs on their sides to provide cover for themselves. The Mounted Police superintendent then sent a small group into some brush on the north side of the road, a larger force of police and volunteers into some woods to the south and anchored the centre of his line with the 7-pound cannon. But even as his men were getting into position, Crozier's scouts came hurtling back through the relative safety of his lines with word of the Métis advance.

As he topped the rise, Dumont instantly saw that Crozier's forces were ready for battle. Dumont's brilliant military mind took in the tactical possibilities of the situation in a matter of seconds: if it came to it, this could be a good place for the Métis to do battle, but he needed to act quickly. Without delay, he ordered his men to take up positions along the ridge of the hillock commanding the gentle slope before him. The position offered the Métis a commanding view of the surrounding territory, while preventing Crozier from moving his cannon atop the rise. In addition, the ridge and the small gully behind it offered his men protection from the artillery.

Dumont then sent some men to occupy a small log cabin to the south of the trail. It was a strong defensive position that, combined with the vantage point at the top of the slope, would stop any potential charge in a deadly crossfire. The police and volunteers in the woods grew edgy when they realized that the Métis occupied the house opposite them. Some thought they heard a gunshot.

"We are being surrounded!" one green-faced volunteer yelled out.

Dumont still aimed to end the day peacefully. He sent forward his own brother, Isidore, and an old Native named Asiyiwin, one of Chief Beardy's headmen, to parley under a white flag of truce. Crozier consented and stepped forward to meet the two, calling for an interpreter as he went. A Half-breed named Joe McKay volunteered and trotted out to accompany the superintendent. Dumont had a good view of the proceedings as the two parties met halfway between the opposing forces, 50 to 60 yards from where he waited.

"Who are you?" Crozier asked, as the two sides met.

"Crees and Half-breeds," Asiyiwin answered bluntly, looking past the uniformed officer to the armed men behind him. It was Asiyiwin who asked the next question. "What do you want with us?"

"Nothing, we only came to see what was wrong," Crozier said hesitantly, unsure exactly how to respond to the question.

At this point the elderly, notoriously near-sighted Asiyiwin turned to Joe McKay, and seeing that he was armed with a rifle and a pistol, produced a mocking grin.

"Where are you going with all those guns, grandson?" the old man chided.

Inexplicably, tragically, old Asiyiwin reached for McKay's rifle, determined to yank it out of the Half-breed's hands. Maybe the Cree was acting as the disapproving elder; perhaps he was hoping to publicly chastise McKay for coming to a parley so heavily armed. Either way, his action was fatally unwise. McKay, unwilling to let the old man have his gun, pulled it back, and a brief struggle ensued. At this point, Crozier gave up on the parley, turned his back on the tug of war and began walking towards his men. He hadn't gone a dozen yards, when McKay panicked, drew his sidearm and pulled the trigger. The first shot of the rebellion rang out in the late morning air and shattered any remaining hopes for a peaceful resolution. Dumont watched Asiyiwin crumple to the ground. And then his eyes turned to his brother, Isidore, who was standing in the middle of an open field in front of 100 armed Canadians.

Crozier raised his arm, and the sound of 100 rifles being cocked reached Gabriel's ears. Isidore had just began to turn away when Crozier gave the order to fire, and Gabriel watched as his brother was cut down. A fierce firefight instantly erupted over the Saskatchewan prairie, and the air soon hung heavy with the acrid scent of gunpowder, bullets, and the cries of the wounded. Dumont shut out all thoughts of his brother and went into battle mode, bending all his energy to the business of killing. He emptied the first 12 ready rounds in *Le Petit* as he moved along the Métis line, encouraging his men and directing their fire. Much to his consternation, Dumont noticed that Riel was also in the thick of the battle. But instead of shooting at the enemy, Riel sat high on his horse, holding his crucifix aloft and praying aloud for the protection of his men.

"Louis!" Gabriel yelled over the sound of battle. "Get down off that horse, or you'll be killed!"

But if Riel heard his general, he gave no indication. Throughout the rest of the battle, he continued his divine exhortations up and down the Métis line, never once breaking the steady litany of his prayer. He punctuated his mantra from time to time with a thundering oath, which every Métis rifleman could hear.

"In the name of God who created us, answer their fire!"

The men in the sleighs had brought iron stove tops with them and were taking cover behind them. Most of the casualties of the battle occurred when the Prince Albert volunteers to the south of the trail rashly tried to charge the log cabin opposite them. Slogging through heavy snow and with no cover, the men were taken down easily by the Métis marksmen. The 7-pound cannon fired two rounds at the stout cabin with little effect. Then, as the over-excited gunner loaded for a third time, he placed the shot in before the gunpowder, effectively silencing the intimidating weapon for the rest of the battle.

This blunder marked the main turning point of the battle. Crozier's men, quickly growing disheartened by the mounting number of their dead and wounded, approached panic when their cannon went down. On the other side, the Métis quickly noticed the silence of the cannon and started to press forward and around the flanks of the Canadian troops, crawling on their bellies as they fired. Dumont was in the thick of it, emptying round after round with devastating effect on the enemy. He advanced steadily, dashing from the cover of one tree to the next, exposing himself for brief intervals as he ran, bullets whizzing all around him.

A young Métis fighter named Joseph Delorme, who worshipped the veteran hunter, stayed right next to him throughout the battle. Running when Gabriel ran, he crouched and fired when Gabriel did, getting closer and closer to the line of Canadian sleds. Joseph was right next to Dumont when a single Canadian bullet struck the Métis general in the head, dropping the stocky man instantly, his blood spraying the tree behind him. Nearly every hunter saw it, and for an instant, a tremor of fear went down the Métis line. Delorme fell to Gabriel's side in a panic, his hands shaking at the sight of his hero lying in the snow, blood pouring freely from his head.

And then Gabriel opened his eyes. The bullet had grazed his skull, taking a strip of scalp with it and knocking him senseless, but he was still alive. Noticing the panicked look on young Delorme's face, he tried his hardest to smile.

"Courage, young Joseph!" Gabriel said. "A man who still has his head is not dead yet!" He then handed *Le Petit* to the young man. "Use this for the rest of the fight; she will serve you better than that," Gabriel said, gesturing to the ancient musket smoking in Delorme's hands.

Dumont struggled to one knee and gave a reassuring wave to his Métis. The relief along the line was almost palpable. He was alive, but it was a grave wound. Dumont realized almost instantly that he had no feeling on the right side of his body. He couldn't move his right arm, and his right leg was numb and heavy.

Clutching his head wound, Gabriel slowly made his way back to the main Métis line, sometimes limping, sometimes crawling and leaving a crimson-stained path behind him. On his way, he found a relative named August Laframboise lying facedown in a blood red slush.

"Damn it, August," Gabriel muttered to himself. "I always warned you against exposing yourself too much."

Dumont winced as he fell to one knee, intending to pray for the soul of the recently departed man. But as he awkwardly tried to make the sign of the cross with his left hand, Dumont lost his balance and fell back to the ground. Slumping down into the snow, the Métis general couldn't help himself; he burst out laughing at his uselessness.

"Cousin," he said, addressing the dead Laframboise, "I shall have to owe it to you."

That was when Edouard Dumont, running low and fast through the snow, finally reached his wounded brother. Having almost lost both brothers that day, Edouard was in a frightful panic. He looked terrified at the long stream of blood that was running down the side of Gabriel's head, and he began dragging him to better cover.

"Gabriel! How are you?" he asked, his voice nearly breaking.

"I'm fine, brother," Dumont responded. "But do not tell Louis that I'm unable to sign the cross." Edouard didn't return his smile. "Enough about me. I'll be fine. It's up to you to direct the rest of this battle."

Louis Riel came running up next, still clinging to the enormous cross. "Uncle! Will you live?"

"Yes, Louis, it seems the Good Lord is content with only my scalp today."

Edouard Dumont assumed command of the Métis just as the Canadians were beginning their semi-organized retreat. Out-numbered, out-gunned and out-manoeuvred, Crozier's force barely managed to retreat in half-decent order, although it might easily have been otherwise. These men had come expecting to send the Métis running before them, and they were now one step away from a full-fledged rout. An enraged Edouard jumped on the opportunity, and roared the second last order of the battle.

"After them! Destroy them!"

The Métis were just getting up to deal the *coupe de grâce* to the retreating men, when they were stopped by none other than Louis Riel. He countermanded Edouard's order.

"We have had enough bloodshed today," Riel called out to the Métis men. "Let them go."

Edouard was about to protest when Riel put a big hand on the man's shoulder.

"Let them go, Edouard. The battle is over; let us go and tend to our wounded."

"Give three cheers, 'hurrah' for Gabriel Dumont!"

Crozier's forces were allowed to retreat in peace. The North-West Mounted Police troops had the courage and presence of mind to take their wounded and most of their dead with them.

But the less-organized, less-cohesive volunteers from Prince Albert, too preoccupied with escaping themselves, left most of their casualties behind. One foolish volunteer named Charlie Newitt whose leg was badly wounded, continued to fire at the Métis after his fellows had quit the field, forcing a group of Dumont's men to subdue him. Captain John Morton, a crack shot who'd killed two Métis during the fighting, had been hit in the back while trying to escape and lay screaming and writhing on the snow. One of Dumont's men gave Captain Morton a mercy killing. The rest of the wounded, however, were picked up and taken back to Duck Lake to be treated.

The Métis had not sought violence, yet the battle of Duck Lake became their stunning success. During the short 20 minutes of the battle, the Métis suffered five dead, including Isidore Dumont and Asiyiwin, who had been killed in the parley before the battle began, and three wounded, including Gabriel. The government casualties consisted of 12 dead and 11 wounded—losses that would have been far greater if not for Riel's merciful intervention. What's more, the Métis accomplished the victory with notably inferior equipment. Many fought with antiquated muskets, while some of the braves arrived with only bows and arrows. And yet they had sent the Canadians—with their cannon, functional rifles and near unlimited ammunition—running back to Fort Carlton. The Métis collected what equipment the Canadians had left behind: eight uninjured horses, five carts, 13 guns and some ammunition.

Dumont's head wound was bound with pieces of cloth torn from a shirt, and the still groggy Métis general had to be tied onto his horse to make the ride back into town. Upon arriving back at Duck Lake, Riel assembled the Métis and gave a short speech.

"The world rained blood!" Riel shouted. He was frazzled by the battle and found himself, uncharacteristically, groping for the next words. Then he remembered Dumont; he turned to his wounded commander.

"Give three cheers 'hurrah' for Gabriel Dumont!" Riel yelled, "and thank God who gave you so valiant a leader!"

The Métis responded lustily, afire with the joy of their victory. Dumont could only weakly acknowledge the cheers.

But Dumont was enraged both by the loss of his brother and cousin and by the government's ready escalation to violence. With blood still seeping down his face from his terrible wound, Dumont demanded to see the prisoners that he had captured before the battle.

He talked loudly in Cree of killing them in retaliation, but, as one of the prisoners later testified, "Gabriel Dumont did not act as a man as though he wanted to kill prisoners very bad. He simply ordered them out of his cabin, and then he seemed to quit there."

Once he had vented his rage on the terrified prisoners, Dumont felt a deep and heavy exhaustion seeping into his bones. He retired to Mitchell's store to clean and dress his wound.

CHAPTER SIX

A Canadian Defeat

"I cannot but consider it a matter of regret."

SUPERINTENDENT CROZIER'S REDUCED AND beaten column limped through the gates of Fort Carlton a few hours after its defeat, just before Police Commissioner Irvine arrived with 83 police officers and 25 Prince Albert volunteers in tow. During the entire return march, Crozier was fearful of how his superior would react to what had transpired. His fears were well founded. Irvine simply couldn't believe the news that greeted him when he arrived at Fort Carlton. He was furious with Crozier.

Irvine icily wrote in his official report on the defeat: "I cannot but consider it a matter of regret that with the knowledge that both myself and command were within a few miles of Fort Carlton, Superintendent Crozier should have marched out as he did, particularly in the face of what had transpired earlier in the day."

Tensions in the region had been running high, and Irvine wondered why on earth Crozier couldn't see that his excursion

Commissioner A.G. Irvine (1837–1916), who led a column of police to Prince Albert in 1885

was the equivalent of putting a spark to the dry tinder of rebellion. Moreover, the superintendent had violated more than one military dictum. His order to march without Irvine led to the division of the Canadian force; he willingly engaged a hostile force of superior numbers; and he allowed the battle to take place on unfamiliar ground that the enemy had chosen. Indeed, according to the rules of engagement, Crozier had practically begged for the defeat he had suffered.

Irvine concluded his report in a grudgingly half-conciliatory tone: "I am led to believe that this officer's better judgement was overruled by the impetuosity displayed by both the police and volunteers."

Crozier's men spent the rest of the day recovering from the battle and caring for their wounded, two of whom died shortly after their return. The very next day, Commissioner Irvine, with the unanimous agreement of his officers, decided to abandon the fort. Their confidence shaken, the once-eager volunteers, anxious to defend their families from what they now deemed to be a most probable Métis attack, were now more than ready to leave the notoriously indefensible Fort Carlton and retreat to Prince Albert. The police could only look at the facts of the situation and agree.

Throughout that day and into the night, the fort was abuzz with preparations for a hurried departure. Makeshift hay mattresses on sleighs were made to carry the wounded. Hudson's Bay factor Lawrence Clarke busied himself taking an inventory of the fort's supplies as the men loaded them for transport. There were far more than they could take, however, so many flour sacks were ripped open and their contents covered in coal oil to keep them from falling into Métis hands.

Later that night, however, a fire accidentally spread through the fort's bunkhouse, and it was all the men could do to remove the wounded before the whole structure was ablaze. Irvine had been worried that Dumont would assemble to ambush his men in the vulnerable "alley" leading out of the fort if he found out they were evacuating. He had thus tried to keep his preparations as secret as possible, even to the point of allowing no one in or out of the fort without special dispensation. Yet suddenly, with the rising flames, the jig was up, and Irvine ordered the evacuations to proceed immediately. After four tense hours, Irvine's disorganized, jittery party began working its way through the forbidding darkness and up the long, dangerously enclosed trail that led them to the relative safety of a hilltop and daylight.

Irvine had good reason to be worried. This was Métis country, and they didn't only know the land, they knew the people. The Métis had eyes and ears in every important location for miles around. Loose networks of scouts and runners relayed information rapidly back to Batoche. Thus, the Métis quickly learned of the fire at Fort Carlton and its hasty abandonment. Métis who were near the fort quickly entered Carlton, put out the flames and saved what provisions they could.

Upon hearing the news, Dumont pressed for action. He knew that the route the men would need to take to Prince Albert offered a perfect spot for an ambush. Morale among the Métis was high, and word of the victory at Duck Lake was spreading all over the country. Dumont knew that a second, even more dramatic Métis victory, tumbling so quickly on the heels of the first, would lead to a possibly irrepressible revolt. The Métis ranks were swelling quickly. They had a large, ready and willing force—limited only by their shortage of arms.

Dumont approached Riel with an idea. "We have some 350 men; 200 are armed. If we ambush the police in the spruce wood around Carlton, we can get more guns and probably capture other supplies from them, too. But we must act now."

The demoralized police and volunteers, loaded down with wounded and all of the supplies from Fort Carlton they could carry, would have been easy pickings for an ambush on ground chosen and prepared by the Métis.

"We could have killed a lot of them," Gabriel later surmised with a touch of regret, and he was probably correct, "but Riel opposed the idea."

"Rebels are good shots."

Thanks to Riel's reluctance to attack, Irvine's column made it to Prince Albert on March 28. A Prince Albert nun watching the men make their way through town observed "almost like

a funeral train did that procession again pass our windows."
The citizens of the town had been worried on March 27,
when they had received word of the defeat of the police and
their volunteers.

"This news," Father André wrote in his journal, "spread terror
in Prince Albert; the inhabitants are maddened by fear. They
expect Riel with his band of Métis followed by the Indians to
pounce upon us and put all to fire and blood."

The sight of Irvine and his men returning did little to allay
the sense of near panic. In other white settlements and forts
across the North-West, the reaction was similar.

But Father André, although he in no way approved of the
Métis resorting to arms, did not fault his flock for the current
situation. "The government of Canada must be severely
blamed and condemned for having brought this war on the
country," he wrote, venting his anger in his journal. "It is their
delay in redressing the grievances of the Métis and their refusal
to listen to the advice given to them that has brought on this
trouble that will end God-knows-how!"

But it appeared that at long last and far too late, the government of Canada was delaying no more. It had slowly been
rousing itself to action even before the events at Duck Lake.
When word that the Métis had begun taking prisoners reached
Ottawa, the government and its supporters tried to downplay
the significance of the events. One Conservative newspaper
wrote of the hostage-taking: "It is of no more consequence
than a petty riot in any well-settled part of old Canada." Publicly,
the government wished to avoid a stir among railway investors
and potential sources of immigration. Privately, however,
Macdonald was more concerned.

Within a week, preliminary arrangements were made to
mobilize Canada's rather humble military. After the British had
withdrawn all but a small garrison at Halifax, the young country
was obliged to defend itself, or at least put up a small show to

that effect. Because the only real military threat could come from the United States, and because Canada had no hope of standing alone against such a powerful force, the country's only hope for protection was from Imperial Mother England. England pledged her aid, but only if Canadians made some sort of effort to defend themselves.

Thus, the Dominion government maintained a small militia that was on the whole poorly trained and equipped and widely dispersed across the country. The small military subsisted on the bare minimum of a yearly budget, grudgingly voted and assigned to it by Parliament. And if the money needed to be spent, those in government felt sure that it should go to their friends. The militia was rife with patronage, because membership in it was seen by most Canadians as more of a badge of prestige and social standing than being part of an effective military force.

The commanding officer of the Dominion's humble military resources had gained his position because his predecessor had, in poor judgement, argued for military efficacy at the expense of patronage. This maverick was promptly persuaded to resign by the minister of militia and defence, Adolphe Caron. The minister found his replacement in Frederick Dobson Middleton.

Middleton was nearing the end of a long career with the British Army. After serving in India, New Zealand and Canada, where he married Montrealer Marie Doucet, he returned to England in 1874 to assume a posting as the commandant of the military academy at Sandhurst. As the term of the position drew to a close, however, Middleton had little to look ahead to and was hard pressed to maintain the appearance of gentility at retired half pay. The position as the commanding officer of Canada's tiny army came almost as a godsend. Middleton fully hoped to do little more than cooperate fully within the government's system of patronage dispensation. He could enjoy a semi-retired life with high social standing in the atmosphere of a colony that worshipped all things British.

So it was on March 23, 1885, that the major general found himself most unexpectedly—three days before Duck Lake—travelling westward with a cadre of aids, laying out strategies for the impending confrontation with the Métis. The Canadian government had become alarmed enough at the turn of events in the North-West to dispatch their highest-ranking officer. Along the way, Middleton called on officers commanding militia units, ordering them to be ready for action. Meanwhile, he claimed to the inquiring press that he was merely travelling on a tour of inspection. When Middleton reached Winnipeg on March 27 and confirmed the rumours of the Mounted Police defeat near Duck Lake, he pressed on to Batoche with the local militia made ready for him at Manitoba's capital. But first he wired Ottawa, requesting that the government mobilize and dispatch the meagre resources of the artillery and infantry schools as well as the best urban militia units.

But Middleton's request would be of no immediate help to the government forces that were frighteningly close to Batoche. Shortly before he abandoned Fort Carlton, Irvine had sent a cautionary telegraph to Edgar Dewdney, the lieutenant-governor of the North-West Territories, requesting the size of the force being sent to the area should be quintupled: "1500 men should be sent in at once." Dewdney forwarded the telegraph to the prime minister immediately, adding one sparse but evocative sentence: "Rebels are good shots."

"If anything happened to Dumont..."

Although slowed by his wound, Dumont was still active in the days following Duck Lake. All of the Métis families in the surrounding countryside moved into Batoche. Natives and

Métis soldiers rounded up every animal they could find; their
allies offered cattle and mounts freely. Those families who did
not support the rebellion had their livestock and horses seized
under threat of violence. As far as Gabriel Dumont was concerned, the Métis were now at war, and he had no problem
treating dissenters as enemies.

Yet at the same time, Gabriel revealed the abiding and fun-
damental humanity that defined him. The day after the Métis
buried their dead from the Battle of Duck Lake, Dumont
approached Riel.

"It is a shame to leave exposed to the dogs the bodies of our
dead enemies. In the end, they bore no more ill will against
us than we against them."

And so, one of the prisoners, Tom Sanderson, was sent to
the Canadian forces while they were still at Fort Carlton. The
envoy carried a letter signed by Riel and bearing Dumont's
mark, guaranteeing safe conduct for the Canadians to bury
their dead.

Irvine was so wary and agitated, however, that he originally
believed the Métis offer to be some sort of ruse. He even briefly
imprisoned the unfortunate Sanderson on the misguided suspicion that he was acting as a Métis agent. Only after they had
reached Prince Albert was Sanderson, with the help of the residents, able to convince Irvine to be allowed to return to collect
the bodies for burial. To better protect them from the elements
and animals, the Métis stored the frozen corpses in the cabin
the Métis had occupied during the battle—the same building
from which so many of the Canadians had been killed. The
Métis even helped in the joyless task of stacking the bodies, like
gruesome cordwood, onto the sleighs that would return the
sad cargo home to a Christian burial.

In the days and weeks following their first victory, the badly
injured Dumont went to work securing the help of those
Native tribes he had established relationships with during the

preceding decades. He dispatched trusted envoys on snowshoe and horseback to the various Métis communities and Native tribes, mighty and not so mighty, across the North-West—the Sioux, Cree, Assiniboine, Stony, Blackfoot and Gros Ventre.

Thus, Dumont took advantage of his more than 20 years as leader of the Saskatchewan Métis. He had travelled far and wide across the great prairies, learned the languages of the Native tribes, come to know them and gained their respect. During these decades Dumont established peaceful ties— through blood relation, rough alliances or non-aggression agreements—with almost every Native tribe in the region. He had sent gifts of tobacco and tea in years of plenty, and during hard times in the 1880s, food. In the preceding year, Dumont was also instrumental in including in the Métis petitions to Ottawa demands for the government to live up to its obligations under the Native treaties it had signed. Furthermore, with Riel, he had organized a meeting of Native chiefs in July of 1884 to secure these relationships.

A more widespread uprising in the North-West would in all likelihood have forced the Macdonald government to the negotiating table. As it was, after the single victory at Duck Lake, a vigorous enthusiasm for revolt spread across the prairie like an early spring. On March 30, a group of Stonies and Chief Poundmaker's Cree sacked the town of Battleford. On April 2, a band of Plains Cree under Chief Big Bear killed nine Canadians in the northern town of Frog Lake and then moved on to successfully demand the surrender of Fort Pitt. No Hudson's Bay Company store was safe. Several across the North-West were plundered as groups of disgruntled Natives started rising up against the Canadian authority. A group of Teton Sioux under Chief White Cap together with a group of Métis who had been living with them arrived at Batoche singing and shouting war cries in the middle of April, swearing their allegiance to Dumont's cause.

Cree chiefs Big Bear (1825–88) and Poundmaker (1842–86), taken in 1886 while they were incarcerated for their part in the North-West Rebellion. Although it is widely believed that both men urged peace for their respective bands, many of the warriors under them were eager to join the Métis during the North-West Rebellion. Big Bear's Cree killed settlers in Frog Lake and razed Fort Pitt, while the Cree from Poundmaker's reserve took Battleford. In the end, both men's forces were defeated. Poundmaker's warriors lost out at the battle of Cut Knife Hill when they faced a force of 325 militia under Lieutenant-Colonel William Otter. Big Bear's braves were likewise defeated when they fought a Canadian force under the command of Major General T.B. Strange at Frenchman's Butte.

Crowfoot, age 57, possibly taken during a visit to Prime Minister Macdonald in Ottawa to speak for Native rights

Yet the unrest was but a small taste of what might easily have transpired. Because the tribes to whom Dumont had sent tobacco smoked it, he knew they would respond to his invitation for assistance. The Natives were indeed receptive, but still cautious. The Métis victory at Duck Lake had tremendous symbolic significance, proving that armed resistance to the government en masse was both possible and may even be successful. In reality, however, the Battle of Duck Lake had been a minor engagement, and so the most powerful of the Native chieftains, Crowfoot of the Blackfoot, Piapot of the Cree and Sitting Bull of the Sioux, judiciously chose to wait and see how events would develop before committing themselves to the high-stakes gamble of open warfare with the Canadian government. The larger Métis communities in St. Albert, Lac Ste. Anne, Wood Mountain and Qu'Appelle were similarly cautious.

The problem with this stance was that Dumont and his men did not have much time to be cautious. Everyone in Batoche knew that Middleton and his massive force of Canadian militia were advancing. Middleton, by all accounts, held the upstart Métis in contempt and was certain they could be dispensed with easily enough. Not without good reason. For as much as Riel and Dumont may have dared to hope, a good many factors weighed against their success.

For just as Chief Crowfoot ordered his mighty Blackfoot Confederacy to remain neutral in the fight against Ottawa, General Middleton's military juggernaught was making its way into the Saskatchewan Valley. In Qu'Appelle, his enormous force had grown to more than 2000 men by early April. Devising a three-pronged strategy to thwart the rebellion, Middleton divided his army, ordering Lieutenant-Colonel William Otter to engage Poundmaker at Battleford, sending another senior officer, Major General Thomas Bland Strange after Big Bear in the north and personally commanding the force that would march to Batoche and meet the Métis led by Louis and Gabriel.

So it was that Middleton's force left Qu'Appelle on a cold April 6 morning—more than 800 soldiers armed with the best weapons of the day and 120 vehicles loaded with supplies and ammunition. The force slowly and deliberately made its way north to Batoche, and with its every step, the anxiety in Batoche increased. The much-talked-of Canadian militia was coming.

Before news of the defeat at Duck Lake hit the streets in the East, the militia had been having a difficult time rousing the support, or even the presence, of its citizen-soldiers. At

Major General Thomas Bland Strange (1831–1925), who led the
Alberta Field Force into action at Frenchman's Butte

first, the bank clerks, shop assistants and mechanics of the East proved less than eager to risk the wrath of their employers on the basis of some mere agitation out in a land of which they knew next to nothing. But their attitude changed soon after March 26, when patriotic calls to duty became the fashion in newspapers across the country. Volunteers were so numerous that many had to be turned away. Excited crowds packed train stations as young men in hastily arranged and unfamiliar uniforms started out on an adventure that soon proved to be far less romantic than they had dreamed.

The rebellion fell almost like manna from heaven into the lap of the Canadian Pacific Railway (CPR). Until then, it had been teetering on the verge of bankruptcy because it was unable to complete large sections of track across the country without more public money. The government could hardly swallow its pride and send its troops across the country to do their patriotic duty on the already completed American railroad lines to the south. Room was quickly found in the public purse to use, and thus save, the CPR. Not that the 1885 militiamen would have objected to using the American rails. These men suffered a dismal march, struggling over long stretches of unfinished track in sleighs and on foot in the still-bitterly cold late winter nights in northern Ontario.

Middleton moved northward to Humboldt and then cut straight west to arrive at Clarke's Crossing on the South Saskatchewan. There, he could ease his overtaxed supply lines by having his men resupplied via the river. It had taken 11 days for Middleton to cover 180 miles, and the exhausted state of his troops, who were completely unaccustomed to such activity, alarmed the major general enough that he camped at Clarke's Crossing for six days.

The Métis in Batoche knew everything there was to know about Middleton's force. Not only did they have scouts following Middleton's column, but they had one of their own men,

Jerome Henry, working as a teamster inside the troop itself. From Henry they received detailed and accurate information on the number, composition, equipment and overall fitness of Middleton's command. Henry even sent sketches detailing the organization of Middleton's encampments, the surrounding terrain, the location of telegraph lines and whatever else he saw.

In early April, when news of Middleton's arrival at Qu'Appelle came to Batoche, Dumont was eager to go out and meet the enemy. He planned to use a guerrilla-style of warfare on Middleton's superior advancing force. Set on using dynamite to destroy the vital railway connection that kept the Canadian army reinforced and supplied, Dumont then aimed to harass the column with nightly raids, attacking under cover of darkness and making off with much-needed supplies. These tactics would have suited the nature of his force perfectly, freeing his men to use their initiative, courage, superior mobility and peerless knowledge of the surrounding country.

Dumont's captains, too, agreed with Dumont's plans. But not Louis Riel. The venerable Métis leader was adamantly against such attacks, somehow convincing himself that the best strategy was to stay in Batoche and wait for the attacking force to arrive.

Riel, flush from the victory at Duck Lake, insisted that more such battles would follow if the Métis retained the moral high ground. Dumont's idea of killing at night and then disappearing into the darkness was repugnant to Louis. He was convinced that they had won the day against Crozier only because God had weighed in on their side, and he argued tirelessly that the Métis should remain upright. Louis' reasoning made little sense to Gabriel, but while the Métis general's frustrations with Riel mounted, so too did a secret hope that Louis was right. Even as every military instinct in Gabriel called for action, his faith in Riel stayed his hand.

"Let us not slink through the darkness like so many serpents, stabbing at their backs when they cannot see us," Riel said. "No, let us stand proudly in front of them under the daylight, soldiers of God, who look their enemy in the face."

And so it was lucky for General Middleton that Louis Riel had so much influence. The Canadian general's soldiers were, for the most part, completely green and far away from the life and land they knew. They had already demonstrated a tendency for jitteriness and panic—especially at night. Nervous watchmen issued challenges and fired shots at little more than shadows and bushes so regularly that the troops got little sleep. Such martial amateurism, combined with the still-cold weather and the marching, made for a life that was substantially less appealing than the dashing, romantic adventure that many had originally imagined. Of course, Gabriel's quick, guerrilla-style raids under cover of darkness would likely have inflicted heavy casualties on the Canadians and offered a rich bounty of captured arms and supplies. These tactical successes would also have aided the Métis strategically, by drawing more reinforcements to the Métis base at Batoche and by encouraging increased involvement from the Native tribes.

Why, then, did Riel oppose these sound plans? It was something that he confided only in his diary—his touching concern for his friend, Gabriel.

"If anything happened to Dumont," Riel confessed after one of Dumont's early appeals for action, "it would not only be a misfortune for his friends, but an irreparable loss for the army and the nation. If Uncle Gabriel were cured of his wound," he continued, "I should be more willing to see him start on an expedition of this kind."

On a basic level Riel was worried for the welfare of his badly injured friend, but he also recognized the importance of Dumont to the Métis rebellion as a whole. If Dumont was killed or injured again, Riel feared that event could be a death knell for the Métis cause.

Riel was, to say the least, a dreamer. Political considerations aside, he had come to see the Métis building a new city of God along the banks of the Saskatchewan. His community would be based on a renewed religious and humane foundation, of which he would be the head. Riel was visited in restless dreams by the forces of good and evil doing battle in apocalyptic confrontations. In Riel's mind the battle was no longer political, but religious. He concluded that the Métis must remain pure of spirit and wait to defend Batoche against the attacking evil.

"I yielded to Riel's judgement," Dumont said later, "although I was convinced that mine was the better plan." But Gabriel deferred to Riel's plan of inaction. Why? As with so many of the questions we ask of the past, the answer may never be fully known, but Dumont did betray several reasons in his later accounts of the rebellion.

Some of Dumont's reasons were personal. Riel's methods were debatable, but the genuine love he had for his people was not. As they had worked closely together over the last year, Dumont, the experienced leader and able judge of human character, had come to know and respect this facet of Riel. Riel's love for the Métis people was the foundation of the strong friendship the two men developed for one another. But Louis Riel was more than just a well-respected friend.

Riel was also a walking legend in the Canadian West, especially so to the Métis. His legendary status lent him a powerful presence among men, a confident charisma that had a way of influencing the most stubborn people. And then there was the self-proclaimed mantle of the prophet that Riel wore. If Dumont was schooled by the hard realities of the Plains, he was also in possession of a fierce Christian faith. But in the end, Dumont's obedience relied on nothing more than unquestioned loyalty. Years later, Dumont would just shrug when people questioned him about his obedience.

"He was my chief."

"Middleton's soldiers would have been lucky to get out alive."

On April 23, however, Dumont would be held in check no longer. He had watched as Middleton advanced methodically toward, and now through, Métis country. He saw Middleton gain in strength and confidence, even as his own men grew restless and demoralized at their own inaction. This time, when he approached Louis Riel about his intention to move on Middleton, Louis knew by the look in his general's eye that he could say nothing to stop him.

"All right!" Riel said, throwing up his hands. "We will do as you wish."

Batoche burst into hurried activity as the Métis prepared for their foray against the enemy. Dumont left 30 men under the command of his brother, Edouard, in the Métis settlement with orders to guard the prisoners and the town in case any kind of action should be mounted against them from Prince Albert. Dumont led 150–200 Cree, Sioux and Métis, most on horseback but some on foot, south along the east bank of the South Saskatchewan. But an anxious Riel slowed their progress. Having decided to accompany the expedition, Riel insisted on regular stops so that he could recite the rosary.

Dumont estimated that his column had only moved about four miles by eight o'clock that night. With darkness falling fast, he decided to stop at Roger Goulet's farm and get his men some food. Two of Goulet's herd were slaughtered and roasted over open fires to satisfy the hunger of his men.

Riel again tried to open the discussion of Dumont's planned offensive action, but as the debate became heated, two messengers came galloping, breathlessly, into the Métis camp. They brought an urgent message from Gabriel's brother. Edouard had heard a rumour that a troop of police had been spotted on the trail from Qu'Appelle to Batoche, and he requested that either Riel or Dumont return with at least 30 men to bolster the defences of the Métis base.

The rumour was actually false and based on earlier reports. Dumont doubted its authenticity, but he kept his reservations to himself, recognizing his brother's request as a blessing in disguise. Riel volunteered to lead the contingent returning to Batoche and asked for not 30 but 50 men. Many of the fighters had left Batoche reluctantly, frightened that their families might be attacked in their absence, so Louis had no problem taking back as many men as he wanted. And the Métis general knew that if the coming battle unfolded as he imagined, it would be a bloody affair and not for the faint of heart. And so Gabriel chose his fighting force, weeding out those men he deemed least reliable.

The mounting frustration that Dumont was feeling with Riel and his relief at Riel's departure, was evident as he set forth with his smaller but more battle-ready column.

"Now that we won't be praying so much," he said to his captains, "we'll be able to move faster." He was now free to set his mind to the task at hand. His initial plan was bold, simple and terrifying. Intending to attack the Canadian camp that night, Dumont planned to light a prairie fire around the sleeping men and then attack while they were reeling from smoke and confusion.

"If we had found the English camp that first night," Dumont said later, "Middleton's soldiers would have been lucky to get out alive."

But Middleton's soldiers were lucky. The Métis were unable to locate the exact location of the Canadian camp before daybreak. Aware he had lost the advantage of surprise with the coming light, Dumont wisely and quickly formed an alternate plan.

"I want to treat them as we would buffalo."

Middleton took the complete absence of any opposition as a sign of defeat, and his imperial arrogance grew as he neared Batoche. He had three captured Sioux in his camp who did nothing but bolster his confidence. They claimed that they had been forced to join the Métis uprising against their will and that Dumont and Riel had only 250 men in their command at Batoche. So confident did Middleton grow, that he fretted the Métis would not even give him enough of a fight to claim a glorious victory. Thus, Middleton tried to entice his enemy into battle by wilfully committing the supreme military blunder: he divided his forces. He sent approximately half of his men over to continue along the left bank of the South Saskatchewan River, while Middleton advanced with the other half along the right bank.

Dumont left his men near the Tourond family's farm, which was nestled above the only sizeable tributary of the South Saskatchewan River between Clarke's Crossing and Prince Albert, and went to scout out the enemy himself. Upon his return, the Touronds generously slaughtered and cooked one of their bulls to provide breakfast for Dumont and his men. Scarcely had they finished their meal, when the Métis received word that Middleton's scouts were approaching. Dumont quickly moved his men to receive their guests. With characteristic and seemingly effortless tactical skill, the Métis general had chosen to engage his enemy at a spot perfectly suited for an ambush, and he positioned his men accordingly.

The Métis called the gully surrounding Little Beaver River, Tourond's Coulee. The English called it Fish Creek, the name by which it is known today. The creek flows in a generally northward direction to merge with the mightier South Saskatchewan on the larger waterway's eastern bank. In 1885, the trail from Clarke's Crossing to Gabriel's Crossing, and points beyond, intersected the creek at Tourond's farm. The trail makes a long, looping turn to the right as it approaches the creek before it turns left again, descends into a ravine and leads across the creek and up past the Tourond's farmhouse. A fair amount of brush and woods grew on the bluffs around the gully, but at this vaguely rectangular spot where the waterway intersected the trail, the ground was more open.

Dumont stationed 130 men in a hollow on the bank of Fish Creek, opposite Tourond's house. From his position, the bulk of his forces would have a commanding view of Middleton's column as it descended the open ground of the trail into the gully. Dumont gathered these 130 around, giving them a quick talk on the importance of discipline in an ambush.

"Do not fire on the Canadians until the front of their column is all the way down to the creek."

He stressed to his warriors who would be on this commanding bluff that they should let all of Middleton's column enter the coulee before they opened fire. His men skilfully found small animal trails and hollows in which to hide and find cover once the fighting began. Dumont also left a small troop of mostly Cree and Sioux in some cover at the bottom of the ravine to block Middleton's way forward and out of the ravine when the shooting began. He then left with 20 riders, looking for cover farther ahead on the trail. He planned to close the trap on Middleton's line with these men, swinging in behind them to block their retreat when the 130 fired the opening shots of the ambush.

"We will not charge until they realize that they are penned in," Gabriel told these horsemen. "I want to treat them as we would buffalo," he said, referring to how buffalo were sometimes slaughtered by driving them into pits or pens and then closing the door behind the herd. The animals were then killed from all sides as they milled about in a panic.

When Middleton's column herded itself into the pen of the coulee, Dumont's men on the bluff, would fire from their commanding and covered positions on the elevated flanks of Middleton's column and slaughter the trapped soldiers.

For all the brilliance of Dumont's plan, the lack of discipline of his men doomed it to failure. Surprise was crucial to its success, and Dumont gave his men express orders to remain out of sight. He told his men not to use the road that cut across Tourond's Coulee, because the tracks they left behind might give away their position. But the order was soon forgotten, and a large group of younger fighters tramped up and down the dirt road chasing Tourond's cattle.

Middleton's Half-breed scouts, riding in advance of the main body, caught site of the tracks on the road and sent word to Middleton. The general halted his march and sent more scouts out to explore the coulee. Major Charles Boulton's volunteer scouts rode forward cautiously. When one of them approached the spot where Dumont and his 20 men were hiding, Gabriel knew the jig was up. It was impossible for a body of 20 men to remain hidden when others were actively looking for them. One man promptly spotted Dumont and his riders in a small wooded hollow behind the sparse cover of the budding spring branches. The scout turned and fled the moment he caught sight of them.

Dumont knew he couldn't let the man raise the alarm and foil his already-compromised ambush. With a determined shout, Gabriel spurred his horse after the lone scout, aiming to catch up with the man and dispose of him as quickly as possible. He very nearly succeeded. Crouching low over his horse, Dumont was gaining ground on the lone scout when a gunshot diverted his attention. He had been concentrating so hard on catching the lone rider that he failed to notice another scout who was coming to the aid of his fleeing comrade. That was when he heard one of his own men calling him.

"Gabriel! Come back or you'll be lost; there are too many of them!" the man shouted, referring to the 40 scouts, who were just spotted farther along the trail.

Realizing then that his carefully planned attack had been foiled, Dumont pulled up his horse, and uttering a string of curses, fired two shots at the fleeing scout and plunged back down towards the coulee and his horsemen.

"Don't be afraid of the bullets, they won't hurt you."

The morning of April 23 began pleasantly enough for the Canadians. They broke camp shortly after dawn under a clear sky. They whistled as they marched, buoyed by a blithe confidence that the coming day would hold no more action than any of the previous days. They made bets over pot shots taken at geese and gophers, believing that this might be their only chance to fire their rifles. While the coming day would put a harsh end to such talk, things could have gone much worse for the clerks and bankers from the East. Middleton, who had been warned of the potential danger of the trail crossing the ravine ahead, pushed his scouts a little farther forward than usual and discovered the obvious signs left behind by Dumont's rash younger men. The information was enough to give even the arrogant Middleton pause. He ordered his scouts to fan out and push still farther ahead into the coulee that lay before them.

Middleton rode forward along the trail with Major Boulton, whose scouts were dispersed in a skirmishing formation around and ahead. Both heard the two shots Dumont took at the fleeing scout. Boulton ordered the 40 men with him to wheel to the left and charge towards the sound. They quickly spotted Dumont's 20 horsemen, who let loose a volley at the charging Canadian scouts and then retreated towards a small gully that fed into Fish Creek. Dumont's men dropped to their feet and slapped their horses, sending the animals running from the imminent fight. Crouching low, the men took cover in the hollow gully. Boulton heard the sound of rifles cocking. He ordered his men to dismount and take cover, but the command came too late. The Métis opened up a murderous fire, killing two of Boulton's men and felling two horses. A hot fire fight quickly ensued, and the air was heavy with the zip and whistle of flying lead.

In a matter of minutes, two more of Boulton's scouts were hit, and Boulton began to fear for his position. Knowing that the withering Métis fire would cut them down if they ran, Boulton decided their best chance was to hunker down and return fire until the rest of the Canadian column arrived on the scene. He hoped they'd still be alive by then. In the excitement that led to the opening shots of the battle, Dumont had become separated from his men. He tied his horse up and went down into the small coulee to get back to them. The first man he stumbled on was a young Native, dug in deep behind a bush and firing at the enemy. Gabriel fell to one knee and began doing the same.

Canadian reinforcements trickled in as the most advanced scouts converged on the battle. Dumont wanted to set a good example for his men and was firing as rapidly as he could.

"I don't know if I killed many men because I took cover immediately after each shot," Dumont later said. "But I couldn't have missed often."

Evidently, Dumont's efforts had their intended effect, as the scouts began to pay special attention to the hollow where Dumont had taken cover. Dumont's thicket quickly turned to lethal ground, when it became the target of a hail of bullets that kicked up dirt, tore leaves and split branches. Knowing that they wouldn't survive a continued barrage, Dumont and the young Native next to him fled the hollow, scurrying out on their elbows and bellies.

After the initial flurry, the remainder of Dumont's horsemen slowed their rate of fire considerably. The Métis were short of ammunition, and each of the rebels had been issued a mere 20 rounds before leaving Batoche. One Sioux brave's courage was not deterred by such practicalities. Eager to exhibit his fear-lessness to the other men, the brave rushed out from his cover and leapt onto open ground. There the young man shouted his war cry and danced from foot to foot, waving a hatchet above his head. Boulton's unit rewarded the man's show of courage with a volley of bullets. The Native fell where he stood, gravely wounded, his chest riddled with Canadian slugs. Meanwhile, Middleton's reinforcements were beginning to arrive from the rear; the general deployed them in a line towards his right and along Fish Creek.

Once Dumont managed to extract himself from the lead-saturated thicket, he ran through the bush, keeping low and moving fast, making his way towards the 20 riders under his command. He first ran into a group of Sioux, who told him of the wounded brave lying just beyond the cover of the bush. The Sioux told him of a wounded man up on the rise, but all Gabriel heard was lost weapons and ammunition—precious supplies for his under-supplied force. Although he probably would never have admitted it in the midst of the rebellion, Gabriel would likely have traded the lives of 20 men for a box of Winchesters and one ammunition belt for each of his soldiers. Dumont crawled forward to relieve the man of his weapons. The brave was lying on his back, the war song he had been bel-lowing just minutes prior now a weak warble on bloodied lips, barely audible over the exchange of gunfire. The only weapon the dying warrior had was an old hatchet clutched tightly in his right hand. Gabriel cursed and crawled back into the bush, leaving the mortally wounded brave to die.

The Battle of Fish Creek raged all through the day on April 23. The muzzle flashes of the Métis riflemen are visible in the lower right corner.

Middleton brought two of his cannons into action, but after a few shots he realized that his opponents were too well covered for his artillery to be effective and ordered the ordnance to stop. In the meantime, most of his men had arrived on the scene. These part-time soldiers were reluctant to move forward into the deadly accurate fire of the rebels, and the Métis could hear the curses of the militia officers as they tried to get their men to advance. And the officers, mounted on their horses, presented irresistible targets to the Métis sharpshooters; more than one man with brocaded sleeves tumbled from his horse before the Canadian line was finally coaxed into its slow advance.

By this time, Dumont had joined up with the 20 dismounted horsemen who were still returning the Canadians' fire from the cover of the small gully. Gabriel tried to move the men to a more defensible position in the copse, but they were effectively pinned down by the enemy fire, which cut through the woods all around them. Vastly outnumbering Gabriel's little force, the Canadian line was spreading out along the clumps of trees on either side of the coulee and was raining down concentrated fire on Gabriel and his small cadre of fighters. One by one, Dumont's men ran, abandoning the exposed position.

Their situation grew so precarious that Dumont's friend, the usually dauntless Napoleon Nault, voiced his frightened thoughts aloud.

"They have the right idea, Gabriel! We should get out of here. This is suicide!"

Dumont couldn't help but see the wisdom of Nault's advice and called a retreat to the men who remained with him. Covering each other as they made their way back to their horses, the Métis riders jumped into their saddles and dashed back towards the main body of troops who were hidden in their positions in the Fish Creek ravine.

Dumont was in for an unpleasant surprise. The far right of Middleton's troops had already come into fighting contact with the 130 warriors Gabriel had left in his strongest position. And while General Middleton was aware that his artillery was ineffective against the well-covered men in the coulee, the Métis did not know this. Realizing that although his cannons couldn't hit the enemy, they still had intimidation value, Middleton ordered his gunmen to keep firing into the ravine. For the vast majority of Dumont's men, it was their first experience with artillery—with the possible exception of the two rounds fired by the seven-pounder at Duck Lake—and the sound and sight of the shrapnel exploding over their heads terrified them. Just 47 of the older Métis, hardened by their experience in the prairie buffalo hunts, remained steadfast in their positions. But when Dumont arrived, he discovered that a large number of the younger Métis had fled, along with almost all the Natives.

Dumont charged after his panicked men, catching up to and rallying 15 of them near Tourond's homestead. The rest were too far gone. The 47 stalwarts in the coulee now faced the brunt of Middleton's advance. The Canadians, who didn't have to worry about ammunition supplies, poured fire liberally into the Métis positions, although, to their frustration, the Canadians had little idea where their well-covered opponents actually were.

"The rebels," Major Boulton later noted with grudging admiration, "would pop up from the ravine, take a snap shot and disappear in an instant."

The Canadian soldiers felt as if they were firing at little more than puffs of smoke.

"This snap fire, however," Boulton noted, "was precisely directed as well as murderous upon all the troops engaged, one poor fellow after another falling, some killed outright, others consigned to the tediousness of the hospital."

Dumont turned to the frightened young men now with him and flashed them a cavalier grin, hoping to ease their panic.

"Don't be afraid of the bullets," he told them above the noise of battle, "they won't hurt you. None of the Canadians can see us; they are only firing into the shadows and praying."

He then showed them how to perform the deadly Métis technique of snap firing, showing oneself only long enough to let loose an accurate shot before quickly taking cover again. Their morale bolstered by their general, the young Métis found it in them to let out a battle cry and followed Dumont, plunging down across the coulee towards Middleton's right flank.

The front of the rebel's position, Battle of Fish Creek, 1885

The Canadian cannon was roaring all this time, but the Canadian artillerymen were having a difficult time of it. They quickly ran out of ready case shot and had to make their own ammunition by pouring gunpowder into hollow cannon balls and inserting fuses of the proper length. In the excited rush to battle, no one had remembered to bring the funnel to pour the gunpowder, so they had to improvise, which took time. Then, to make matters worse, they found their fire to be practically useless, except for the panic that it caused among some of Dumont's troops. The gunners were unable to depress their cannons to fire down into the coulee, so their shots passed harmlessly over the heads of the Métis.

An enterprising lieutenant sized up the situation and seized the initiative. He had his men pull a cannon up to the edge of a bluff above the Métis right, giving them a commanding view east into the valley. The men tilted the muzzle of the threatening weapon downward by hand and commenced firing into the valley allowing for more direct fire on the Métis positions. However, the poor gunners, perfectly silhouetted and exposed atop the bluff, offered tempting targets to the Métis marksmen down below. After suffering heavy casualties, the gunners were compelled to retreat.

Dumont advanced cautiously towards the enemy lines and to the left of his brave 47 who stubbornly refused to budge. Dumont caught sight of one officer firing into the coulee and promptly took him out of the fight with a single shot to the shoulder. The young men with Dumont laughed at the wounded man's cries of pain, causing another soldier to poke his head over the lip of the ravine to get a look at the attackers. *Le Petit* sounded again, and that soldier slumped over dead with a bullet between his eyes. Dumont, the warrior who had been held in check by a hesitant Riel for too long, was restrained no more. Today he would fight without mercy. He continued firing on the soldiers above, two of his companions making sure the expert marksman had a steady supply of cartridges.

Even so, Dumont and his group of 15 men were rapidly running out of ammunition. When they were down to seven bullets among the entire group, the general came up with an alternate plan. Noting that the Canadians were downwind, Gabriel reasoned that if he set fire to the prairie grass, the flames and smoke would force the enemy to withdraw. He might then even be able to advance under cover of smoke and pick up what arms and ammunition they might abandon in their flight.

He hollered his intentions to his men. "We are going to start a fire line in front of the police. When the fire catches I want you to sweep forward right behind the flames, yelling and screaming."

A small contingent of Gabriel's men advanced with him, and just as he ordered, set the dry grass on fire. The moment the fire grew large enough to obscure vision, the Métis advanced, whooping and hollering. Just as Dumont had predicted, the Canadians believed the Métis were counterattacking, and the troops closest to the wall of flame turned and fled. Gabriel and his men pushed up over the lip of the ravine, where they found many dead militia. But Dumont's main objective was foiled because most of the bodies the Canadians left behind had already been stripped of their weapons and ammunition.

The situation alarmed Middleton. "I galloped across to the right," the Canadian general later wrote, "where I could hear heavy firing and saw large clouds of smoke rising. I found that the enemy, reinforced from their centre, was making a determined attempt to turn our right. They had set fire to the prairie and were advancing, firing under cover of the smoke which was rolling up towards us in thick clouds."

Middleton didn't have it exactly right. Dumont's men had precious little ammunition left to fire, and he certainly hadn't had the privilege of any reinforcements to the centre of his line. Dumont had also lost contact with his nearly 50 men fighting in the bluffs above the trail. Indeed, Middleton wasn't sure what was happening on his right flank, having lost contact with the men who were fleeing from the fire. It was at this moment that Middleton's imperial arrogance towards the Métis melted away. Middleton would never again underestimate his opponent.

Clouds gathered in the sky as the day wore on, and at approximately three in the afternoon, rain and sleet began to fall. The sudden downpour, combined with the prompt action of a group of teamsters who had come up from the rear to beat out the flames, extinguished the threatening fire and sent Dumont's interlopers scurrying back into the cover of the ravine.

"I cannot let them be killed without going to their aid."

The attack on the Canadian right had been checked, and Dumont was forced to retreat, all the while worrying about the 47 men positioned in the original ambush site above the trail. He could see that the enemy troops now formed a unified body and were concentrating their attentions on the men trapped in the ravine. As desperate as the situation was, Gabriel saw a potential opportunity. He gathered the men who had charged behind the fire around him, crouching low in the cover of trees around their leader.

"Now that the Canadians have formed a solid line," he told his men, "we will get behind them so that we can save those trapped to our right."

Dumont hoped that this strategy might deceive the Canadians into thinking that they were being dangerously outflanked and thus force them to withdraw some of their troops. He hoped the diversion might allow his imperilled men to escape. But the Sioux warriors who were with him refused to follow.

One of the braves spoke for the rest of Sioux. "If you leave us, we shall run away."

Dumont tried to reassure his men that his plan was plausible, but got no takers. Shaking his head in disgust, the Métis general managed to convince the braves to wait long enough for him to scout out the situation. He moved forward, making it to the edge of the coulee, where the Canadians were firing down on the Métis by the trail. He could clearly see the groups of militia huddled around what cover they could find, pouring a steady fire down on his countrymen below. When Gabriel made a move to break through the line and join the beleaguered Métis, he was instantly spotted and received a hard barrage of fire for his efforts. Unable to join the men in the ravine, Gabriel returned to the youngsters waiting for him in a clump of trees on the prairie. When he got back, he discovered that the Sioux had made good on the brave's warning and had run off, leaving Gabriel with a mere seven Métis fighters.

The sun was beginning to set, and an anxious Gabriel Dumont surveyed the scene. He could see even from a distance that, while his trapped men were still fighting, they were almost completely surrounded by enemy riflemen, who were raining down a ceaseless stream of bullets and grapeshot into the ravine. With only seven men and a handful of bullets at his disposal, Dumont could do precious little. He pulled the men with him out of the cold and wet and took them to Tourond's farm, a little farther up the trail towards Batoche. The famished men helped themselves to Tourond's larder, but Gabriel was in no mood to eat. The boom of cannon and crack of rifle fire had his stomach tied in knots, and the men at the bottom of the ravine possessed his thoughts. Gabriel Dumont, the definitive man of action, was out of options.

The sounds of the battle could be heard all the way to Batoche, and Edouard Dumont grew more concerned as the day wore on. That the rumbling thunder of the Canadian cannon continued hour after hour did not bode well for the Métis combatants at Fish Creek, and Edouard wasn't coping well with the scenarios his dark imagination was producing. He begged Riel to send men to reinforce his brother. Riel refused, telling Edouard that as long as the people of Batoche prayed to God with true faith, no harm would come to Gabriel and his men. Riel himself was in the middle of a marathon prayer session. He had spent the entire day standing in the same spot, facing Fish Creek with both arms extended on either side in the shape of a cross, shouting fervent oaths into the sky. When his arms were too tired to remain raised, women took turns holding them in position.

In late afternoon when the sounds of battle showed no signs of abating, Edouard decided he couldn't rely on Louis' faith for his brother's life. He stormed over to where Louis was standing, still lashed on his imaginary crucifix. Although Edouard was set on what he wanted to do, he was still uneasy about confronting Riel, the Métis holy man. Nevertheless, he found his voice.

"When my own people are in peril, I cannot remain here," Edouard said. "My brothers are there, and I cannot let them be killed without going to their aid."

Riel didn't respond and didn't miss a single word of his continuing prayer, while the younger Dumont gathered the fighting men in Batoche. In a matter of minutes, Edouard was galloping off to Fish Creek with 80 men behind him.

The men in the coulee had a difficult day of it, but the sun was sinking low on the horizon and still they refused to be broken. At about noon, already running short on ammunition, they had given up on any kind of offensive operation and decided to hold their fire for the periodic attacks the Canadians launched down the ravine. On one such occasion, a volunteer force tried to charge the position that the Canadians had dubbed "the hornets' nest." The deadly accurate fire of the experienced Métis hunters dropped eight men, and the charge was quickly aborted. This costly trial convinced an increasingly pessimistic Middleton of the futility of any more such charges, and he refused subsequent officers requesting the honour of leading another rush into the ravine. The day wore on, bringing with it rain and sleet in the afternoon, soaking the combatants through and chilling them to the bone.

As for the Métis, their situation was even bleaker. They were surrounded and knew it. They believed that the rest of the Métis force had either been killed or captured. The best they thought they could hope for was to wait and try to escape under cover of darkness. These men were brave, the best of the Saskatchewan buffalo hunters, but they were not superhuman. Many of the Métis prayed earnestly or quietly recited the rosary. To keep up their spirits, others sang old Napoleonic battle songs passed down to them by their grandfathers or the ballads of their own

Métis bard, Pierre Falcon. Trapped without food, they passed around a pipe that they smoked to defy their hunger.

Then, with light fading from the sky, Gabriel and Edouard Dumont came riding down over the crest of the ravine. Gabriel had ordered his men to spread out and make a lot of noise to frighten off any remaining Canadian troops. The arrival of the riders seemed like a miracle to the trapped Métis. Some who started grumbling against a commander they believed might have abandoned them to their fate, raised their voices in great shouts.

"Gabriel is coming! He rides down for us!"

The arrival of the fresh contingent signalled the end of the battle for the Canadians. Middleton decided that he'd had enough of these rugged opponents for the day. Indeed, the Canadian troops were just beginning to withdraw to their evening camp when Dumont's charge arrived. Some troops were put to flight, and the Métis captured one of the Canadian doctors' kits, which included a bottle of medicinal brandy. A joyous reunion occurred when the last of the Canadians was driven away, and the men from the coulee emerged upon the prairie. Uncorking the brandy, Gabriel offered a toast to Middleton's health, took a swig and passed it around. The long day's fighting at Fish Creek had at last come to an end.

CHAPTER SEVEN

Gabriel on the Battlefield

"We should have been attacked in the ravine and probably wiped out."

MIDDLETON TRIED TO PUT ON the best face he could muster regarding the events at Fish Creek. In his account of the campaign of 1885, he declared, "Personally, I was fairly satisfied with the affair." Almost all of the journalists covering the affair loyally followed suit; they either proclaimed a Canadian victory or chose to focus on individual episodes of Canadian heroism. The facts of the battle, however, told a different story.

The Canadians lost 50 men dead or wounded in the battle, or roughly one in every eight soldiers that had been involved in the fighting. Métis casualties were remarkably light: four dead, two wounded. Much more damaging was the slaughter of the 50 Métis horses tethered at the bottom of the ravine. The loss of these mounts greatly reduced Métis mobility, but Dumont, with an effective fighting force of barely 50 men—all woefully short of ammunition—had checked the advance of a fully equipped and supplied army of several hundred supported by artillery.

Condescension towards their Half-breed foe vanished from the Canadian ranks in a single April day. Major Boulton recounted that in no way could he "disparage the bravery of the enemy." Admiration for the tough Métis was shown, too, in the consistent exaggeration of their numbers and abilities. Middleton, perhaps in an effort to make the engagement seem more successful, fantastically overestimated the casualties the Métis suffered to be 14 dead and 18 wounded. Moreover, both he and Boulton claimed that Dumont commanded a force of more than 300 men whereas, at its strongest in the very early morning, the Métis force numbered about half as many.

To account for the incredible tenacity of the 47 Métis who took the worst the Canadians had to give and held their ground, soldiers, officers and journalists alike claimed that they had fought from within carefully constructed rifle pits. So frustrated had the Canadians been by the effective Métis technique of "snap firing" that they believed the Métis must have prepared trenches and wood-and-earth bunkers in the ravine hours before the battle. Middleton wrote of having seen cleverly constructed rifle pits with his own eyes. In reality, the Métis had not brought any shovels or entrenching tools with them, but they simply made skilful use of the existing terrain, per-haps reinforced in spots by a few loose logs lying close to hand.

After witnessing the Métis' impressive martial ability, Mid-dleton's view of his opponents' skill changed dramatically. After the battle, the major general wired Minister of Militia and Defence Adolphe Caron about the near ambush at Fish Creek: "Their plans were well arranged beforehand, and had my scouts not been well to the front, we should have been attacked in the ravine and probably wiped out."

The old Victorian soldier's assessment was as frank as it was accurate. Had Boulton's scouts not detected Dumont's ambush, Middleton's column would have wandered straight into the killing zone that Dumont had prepared. Their only hope of escape would have been a panicked rout off the right side of the path and down into the rough terrain of the ravine. The Métis would then have been free to pursue the remnants of the column, cutting them down from behind in their terrified flight. The Canadian artillery would never have had the luxury of setting up. It would have been a slaughter.

Nor could Lord Melgund and the other half of Middleton's forces on the opposite side of the Saskatchewan River have come to their rescue until it was too late. As it was, it took several hours for the officers on the other side of the river to organize a frantic and dangerous crossing so they could join Middleton's fight.

The Winnipeg Times was the only Canadian paper to report negatively of the outcome of the battle. "A DEFEAT" ran its headline, which was surrounded by a heavy black border. Yet even the Winnipeg paper dared not speculate on how devastating the defeat might have been if the Métis had actually been able to execute Gabriel's plan and how narrowly Middleton's men had actually avoided such a disaster.

Middleton seemed happy to have the day draw to a close. He made no attempt to pursue or even to scout out the Métis, and he even explicitly ordered his retreating men not to engage Dumont's 80 charging horsemen at the end of the battle. During the night, as the storm settled in, and rain and sleet turned to a heavy snow, a sombre mood descended on the Canadian encampment. Tired sentries paced their watch, nervously expecting the Métis to follow up with a night raid, while in the background, chilling screams from the amputation tent pierced the air.

"If this is God smiling, I'd hate to witness His laughter."

Dumont was in terrible pain. While the warrior's blood had coursed through his veins in the heat of battle, the Métis leader had summoned the will to ignore the injury he'd received at Duck Lake. But during the battle, the festering head wound had re-opened, and as he and his men turned their backs on Fish Creek, a flowing mess of blood and pus streamed from his head and down his face. Dumont had been hardened by a life filled with its share of discomfort and pain, and not a man in the North-West could claim that he had ever heard Gabriel gripe about any physical hurt or ache. And on the evening of April 24, as the freezing rain soaked into the gaping gash on Gabriel's scalp, the only man who heard the grizzled hunter's stifled moans of pain was his brother, Edouard, who rode next to him. As concerned as Edouard was, he dared not ask his older brother about the wound—knowing that Gabriel would be insulted.

Initially, Gabriel was adamant about continuing the fight with a night raid on the Canadian camp. But it quickly became apparent that on this night, few of his men could have summoned the energy for such an action. More than a third of Dumont's men had spent the entire day fighting. They were completely exhausted and, thanks to the pouring rain, soaked to the bone and freezing cold. They were all but out of ammunition, and Dumont himself was fighting off vertigo attacks as alternating waves of pain and nausea radiated through his head. He spread the word for his men to rally at Tourond's farmhouse, and upon arriving there, he discovered that five of his men had already chosen to return to Batoche of their own accord. He finally admitted to himself then that the fight was over for the day; his Métis needed to rest. He made sure his hungry men who had fought in the coulee were fed, and he organized wagons to carry the wounded to Batoche. He ordered a group of younger Métis to escort the wagon train back.

"I wish I was well enough to do it myself," he said to his men, "but I want the rest of you to stay with the wagons. I'll make it back to Batoche on my own."

With these words, the mighty general spurred his horse into a trot and departed alone. Gabriel Dumont, who was practically born to the saddle, now found it took nearly all of his concentration to will himself to stay conscious through the pain and remain astride his horse. He couldn't believe his eyes when, only one half-mile from the Tourond's, he spied two of the men he'd ordered to stay with the wounded coming upon him.

"Where are you going?" Dumont asked, exasperated and angry. "I told you to stay with the wounded. You can see I am not well, but if you leave, I will have to return and ride with them."

The two bowed their heads and returned to escort their wounded comrades.

Dumont's anger was roused yet again when he came upon the five men who had departed before he gave his order. He gave the pain in his skull voice and berated them bitterly from the darkness. The men jumped at the sound of their angry leader's voice. One of the five was Napoleon Nault, a good friend of Gabriel's. Nault had just begun to explain himself when Dumont suddenly appeared out of the darkness, pale as bone, bleeding heavily and swaying dangerously in his saddle. Nault instantly cut himself short and tore off a piece of his saddle blanket to bind his friend's wound as best he could.

With help, Dumont made it back to Batoche shortly before dawn. One of the men looked after his horse, and the general slumped down on the nearest bed for a well-deserved rest. But his sleep was soon interrupted by Riel, who woke the exhausted man with a single gentle nudge.

"What news of the battle, Uncle?" an eager Riel asked. "Was God smiling on us again?"

"If this is God smiling, I'd hate to witness His laughter." Gabriel painfully propped himself up into a sitting position and recounted the day's events to his leader, who was sitting on a chair at the foot of his bed. Gabriel held more than one silent grudge against Louis Riel at this point, angry that Louis had talked him into standing down for so long, disappointed in himself for letting a man who knew nothing of military matters lead him into the current pass.

There was no God at work at Duck Lake or Fish Creek, Gabriel thought to himself, *only the ire of men, a steady rifle hand and the will to win.*

Nevertheless, he told Louis of all that had transpired, and years later, would attribute the dubious "victory" at Fish Lake to Louis' prayers.

His duty to his leader fulfilled, he found his mind alert again after Riel's visit and unable to let go of the day's battle. Sleep refused to come. He was revisited again and again by the horrible hours when he had waited helplessly with a handful of men, armed only with the hope that reinforcements might arrive from Batoche that would allow him to rescue the hunters trapped in the gully.

...but alas for human expectations and vanity.

For the first time in the entire campaign, Middleton seemed to take a step back from engrossing himself in the details of the operation and realize the enormity of the task that faced him. He was leading an army of eager but exasperatingly raw soldiers and officers, its supply lines stretched to the limit, against an enemy that intended to fight—with cunning, determination and skill—on their home territory. Middleton suddenly felt his age. Drained of energy after the Battle of Fish Creek, he had to rely on the help of Lord Melgund to appoint and instruct the night watch, a task which he had always taken pleasure in performing personally—with no shortage of ceremony or even brevity.

His confidence ebbed. The Métis had apparently insinuated rumours into the Canadian encampment that they had prepared smaller ambushes for the advancing army all the way from Fish

Creek to Batoche. In the light of what he had experienced on April 24, Middleton swallowed the bait. He fearfully wired his boss, Adolphe Caron, in Ottawa: "Half a dozen men so positioned could kill a hundred or two without difficulty. It would take a force of five or six thousand men to turn them out."

So taken aback was the major general by his apparent defeat that for two days no one ventured forth into the gully they had driven the Métis from at considerable cost. Indeed, no one in the camp could really claim that ground was in Canadian control. Nor did Middleton even bother to retrieve the bodies of two casualties that the Canadians had left behind in the confusion and shock of their retreat. Certainly there would be no more talk of dividing his forces so as to entice his Métis foe. Middleton resolved to stay just where he was and await reinforcement and resupply by boat via the South Saskatchewan River.

The *Northcote*, the steamer heading down the South Saskatchewan with 80 men and two barges filled with provisions, left Qu'Appelle on April 23 and was beset by difficulties with sandbars. It took much longer than expected to arrive—14 days instead of five. During that time, Middleton began to regain his confidence. Some of Boulton's men had scouted the trail ahead to Batoche and reported that they could see no signs of prepared Métis ambushes. Middleton cautiously rode forward to check out these reports himself and had to agree. Grumbling had begun among the Canadian officers and men during their two weeks of inaction, and Middleton could no longer justify his caution to himself or anyone else. So when the *Northcote* arrived on May 5, the major general finally ordered his column to advance.

By May 7, all of Middleton's force reached Dumont's Crossing, only a few miles from Batoche. Here scouts thoroughly plundered Gabriel and Madeleine's home of any trinkets and clothes left there. The practice was actually a common one for advancing Canadian troops and one condoned by Middleton, who viewed these acts as the normal "usage of war." Livestock was especially vulnerable, but they stole other possessions as well. Dumont's house merited special attention. Soldiers claimed Gabriel's prized billiard table as booty and ripped out planks from his home and nailed them to the sides of the *Northcote* to provide it with improvised armour. What remained of the Dumont homestead was put to the torch.

From Dumont's Crossing, Middleton proceeded cautiously. Still mindful of what had befallen him at Fish Creek, and having heard of several potentially dangerous places on the river trail ahead, Middleton rode forward with a large body of scouts to reconnoitre the area personally. Satisfied, the major general ordered his small army to move forward a few miles to a point a little over halfway towards Batoche. Middleton then scouted forward for the next day's march.

"I still believe to this day that Riel had had a revelation."

News of the destruction of his homestead hit Dumont hard, but then he had seen it coming. Holed up in Batoche, he realized that it was only going to be a matter of time.

Riel, with his perpetual faith and optimism, wrote in his diary a few weeks before: "I saw Gabriel Dumont. He was troubled and ashamed. He wasn't looking at me. He was looking at his table, which was completely bare. But Gabriel Dumont is blessed," Riel continued. "His hope and confidence in God will be justified. He will emerge from the struggle loaded with the booty from his enemies."

For his part, Dumont was not burdened with such illusions. The ever-practical Gabriel swallowed the news of the destruction of his home and focused on the task at hand. All around, he saw work that needed doing, and even though his wound continued to bother him, the tough Métis busied himself in preparation of Batoche's defences. Dumont did not plan any more offensive operations. Riel had interpreted the loss of the 50 Métis horses at the coulee as a divine act.

"O my Métis Nation!" Riel wrote in his diary, taking the voice of God, "For a long time you have offended Me with your horse races, by gambling on these detestable races. That is why, says the Eternal Christ, I killed your horses yesterday while sparing you. O my Métis people! I am only punishing you lightly. All I ask from you is obedience."

Believing God had thus revealed his displeasure in the Métis penchant for horse races, Riel called for four days of fasting, prayer and penance. And the Métis, Gabriel included, obeyed.

Dumont tended to the Fish Creek casualties. He saw his four dead buried at the Church of St. Antoine on the outskirts of Batoche and checked in on the wounded Métis. Madeleine Dumont was caring for the wounded; she told her husband of a disturbing incident that took place in the makeshift Batoche hospital. The Canadian prisoners captured by the Métis had also been obliged to care for the wounded, and one day Madeleine had found a badly wounded Métis warrior in terrible shape because of the ministering of the prisoners. Madeleine discovered that these men had let the patient fall out of bed, and a piece of his skull had broken off and lay on the floor under his bed. As a result, Gabriel and Madeleine were convinced that the English prisoners were responsible for the deaths of several wounded Métis.

"I informed Riel that it would be foolish to use the English prisoners from now on for the hospital work," Dumont later recalled. "Besides, the Natives wanted to kill them every time they met them, and I did not want to take the responsibility of protecting them any longer, after this discovery."

Riel acceded to Dumont's wishes in this matter, and the prisoners were kept confined in an improvised jail. From now on, the Métis would care for their own wounded.

Then one day, not long after the beginning of the fast that Louis Riel imposed on the Métis, an event took place revealing a great deal about the workings at Batoche during the difficult days of the rebellion. Riel spoke up at a meeting of the Métis council about a vision that had visited him. The Métis had deposited a small group of men across the river from Batoche under the command of Albert Monkman. Riel had been out on a patrol with the men in the direction of Duck Lake earlier in the day, and he said he'd had a premonition.

A voice spoke to him: "The man who commands on the other side is going to betray us, because he has suggested to some of them to desert with him."

Riel asked Dumont to investigate this matter, which he did faithfully. Gabriel crossed the river and addressed all of the men bluntly with Riel's suspicion. The men appeared uncomfortable and refused to answer their general directly. Uncertain of the nature of Riel's vision, Dumont decided not to press the matter, but he returned to Batoche and informed Riel about what had transpired.

Louis told Gabriel that he wanted to cross the river himself and address the men on the other side as soon as possible. Gabriel crossed the river again, this time accompanied by Riel. The pair gathered the men together.

Riel spoke, "My friends, I know that someone has suggested to you that you desert. You have refused to reveal this to Mr. Dumont. But rest assured that I shall find out the truth, even if I have to have the suspect shot."

The threat hung in the air after Riel finished speaking, and a heavy silence descended on the men. Everyone, including Gabriel, held his breath. No one expected such words to come from Louis Riel. Patrice Fleury broke the stifled quiet.

"It's true," Fleury said. "Monkman suggested that I desert."

Garçon Abraham Bélanger, Jr., then stepped forward and seconded Fleury's assertion. Riel's premonition had been correct.

Gabriel and Louis crossed back across the river and took the question of what to do about Monkman to the Exovedate. It was decided that Monkman should be placed under arrest. Gabriel himself went out to arrest Monkman personally. He presented him to the council, accompanied by the two witnesses, Patrice Fleury and Garçon Abraham Bélanger. Standing before the council, Gabriel challenged Monkman to respond to the accusations of Fleury, Bélanger and Riel.

"It is true," Monkman replied, "but I did not intend to desert; it was simply to find out if Riel was psychic."

The room came to life with a buzz, as the councillors stared in disbelief at the accused man standing before him, wondering if he actually expected them to believe his flimsy excuse.

"Whatever your reasons," Dumont replied, "I am making you my prisoner."

Monkman blanched. "You are going to do me harm."

Dumont wasn't hearing any sort of supplication. "You have nothing to say in the matter. Although you are Métis, you are now a prisoner of the Métis, for daring to even think of betraying your people."

Dumont then had Monkman bound and placed with the other prisoners.

Riel had many such visions during the rebellion. He was practically besieged by them, and his diaries from the time of the Battle of Fish Creek are filled with interpretations of dreams rich in quasi-biblical symbolism and long imploring prayers for God to aid the Métis nation.

Riel's theological wanderings had escalated. He had become convinced that the Roman Catholic Church had become corrupt and that a new church needed to spring forth from the New World. The idea may seem far fetched now, but the charismatic Riel held such sway among the Métis that even hard-headed men such as Dumont readily, if not always unquestioningly, believed in the power of Riel's visions and submitted to them.

Dumont, however, would never be able to trust military matters to Louis' mysterious premonitions. And while Riel was busy praying and pouring over his diaries, convincing himself that if the Métis were pure, God would not let Batoche fall, Gabriel was not ready to give up the defence of his people to such mystical forces. Again the same conflict arose between the two men. Gabriel pushed for raids, eager to go out and attack the advancing Canadians in small ambushes from wooded copses along the route to Batoche. Riel, on the other hand, was seriously waiting for some sort of divine intervention to rescue the Métis from impending disaster. He urged the Métis to build and maintain their fortress of God, both militarily and morally, at Batoche. Again, it would be Riel's strategy that carried the day.

And so Dumont oversaw the fortification of Batoche. This time, he and his men really did dig rifle pits. Each pit was about three feet deep and perhaps six feet wide, heaped with a small ridge of earth on the left and right to offer some protection from any flanking fire and fronted by two thick logs piled one atop the other. A small sloped trench led out of the back of each rifle pit allowing men to come and go while still offering some protection. A horizontal slit between the front logs provided just enough space for rifles to be fired while still keeping their marksmen well covered. Two or three Métis could man each pit and fire on the enemy with near impunity because the pits were impervious to anything but a direct artillery hit or a drastic outflanking.

Dumont positioned the rifle pits in several staggered lines, which meant that each pit had a field of vision that overlapped at least two other pits in its zigzagging line. Thus, the men in these pits could properly support each other with fire if under attack, and the positions would be difficult to outflank. Having several lines was an additional tactic that allowed the Métis to retreat from forward positions if they were in danger of being captured and to resume their fighting in equally defensible positions to the rear.

They needed every advantage they could get. At the end of April, Dumont had mustered about 160 Métis and Natives under his command as many of the deserters from the Battle of Fish Creek trickled back into Batoche. The numbers were hardly encouraging. Middleton also received reinforcements when Colonel Irvine joined his army with 150 Mounties, bringing the Canadian fighting force to roughly 950 men, which wasn't even the worst of the news. The biggest problem facing the Métis was their severe shortage of ammunition. Down to almost no bullets, the riflemen scoured the countryside in their spare time, looking for anything that could be fired from a rifle—they collected nails, stones and metal fragments.

The odds were bad, and all the Métis knew it, but they fought anyway. They fought for their traditions, their way of life, their rights. They fought for Louis Riel. They fought for Gabriel Dumont.

Dumont was gambling that he could trap the Northcote…

On May 9, Middleton prepared for the final leg of his advance on Batoche. At the same time that his foot soldiers were approaching Batoche, the *Northcote*, armoured with pieces of Dumont's erstwhile home and carrying 30 soldiers, was to proceed down the South Saskatchewan River to provide a diversion and perhaps some trouble on the Métis flank next to the river. Thus, by water and land, the Canadians set off on a final push for Batoche.

But Métis intelligence and Dumont's judgement was sharp as usual. When Dumont heard how his house had been turned into armour for the *Northcote*, he immediately realized what his counterpart intended. Dumont displayed his typical tactical

The steamer, the *Northcote*, that brought provisions to Middleton's men during the Battle for Batoche

ingenuity and daring, as he quickly devised a plan to turn the diversionary attack to his advantage. The Métis general positioned two small groups of men on opposite sides of the South Saskatchewan where the river turned and narrowed just as it approached Batoche. The men were told to fire on the boat when it reached that point. Dumont hoped that this fire would distract the boat's crew sufficiently that it would float downstream into a trap. Dumont then had an iron ferry cable stretched across the river and gave orders that it be lowered to "catch" the *Northcote*, which could then either be captured or destroyed at the Métis' leisure.

Dumont was gambling that he could both trap the *Northcote* and deal with Middleton's forces approaching overland. The potential rewards compared to the risk of the manoeuvre were simply too tempting to ignore. Not only would the capture of the *Northcote* be a morale-boosting victory at a crucial time, immediately before the Métis stand at Batoche, but it might well yield up more arms and ammunition of which his men were so desperately short.

Things worked out better than Dumont could have hoped. Middleton had planned to have his army arrive at Batoche at the same time as the river diversion, but he miscalculated the time needed for his troops to march the distance. The *Northcote* thus arrived in Batoche with uncharacteristic punctuality, at 8 AM as pre-arranged, but instead of a diversion, she was the only show in town. The Métis opened fire and caught the boat in vicious crossfire. Bullets crashed into the wood of the *Northcote* from both sides, sending showers of splintered wood flying over the deck. The boilers and engine had been protected with planks from Dumont's house, but the Canadians had mysteriously neglected to do the same for the wheelhouse, which was invitingly exposed atop the steamer.

The steamer's civilian captain, James Sheets, soon found bullets from both sides zipping and zinging their way through the thin boards around him, turning his wheelhouse into what looked like a large wooden sieve. Captain Sheets wisely embraced discretion and decided that this would be a fine time to lie on his belly and inspect his boat's floorboards, leaving the *Northcote* with no one at her helm. Thus, she drifted aimlessly downstream towards the waiting cable.

Dumont stationed himself halfway between the men on the South Saskatchewan to the west and those in rifle pits to the east, so as to be equidistant from both theatres if Middleton arrived at the same time as his men were trying to capture the *Northcote*. At first, he couldn't keep himself from grinning at the sight of the distressed *Northcote*, but his grin quickly faded when he noticed that Isidore Dumas, the man in charge of the ferry cable, had not lowered it enough to stop the boat. Dumas apparently believed that the cable was low enough and stood waiting eagerly for it to catch the craft. An alarmed Gabriel Dumont jumped on the nearest horse and raced towards Dumas, yelling at him to drop the cable. He was too late. The cable caught the top of the boat's mast and tall smokestack, tearing through and starting a small fire on board, but the prize herself continued to float downstream.

The plucky crew managed to extinguish the fire, despite being shot at whenever they showed themselves on deck. Regardless, the *Northcote*'s less than heroic part in the North-West Rebellion came to an end. A short distance downstream, Captain Sheets stopped the boat and weighed anchor to make repairs. Major H.R. Smith, the officer commanding the troops on board, wanted to turn the *Northcote* around, head back upstream and rejoin the battle he could now hear raging at Batoche. Captain Sheets and his civilian crew did not quite see eye to eye with Major Smith, however, and because the ship's captain was ultimately in charge of anything and everything that happened on deck, the *Northcote* continued on its way downstream to Prince Albert.

"I have already been close enough to take a shot in the head."

As Middleton approached Batoche, he and his men could hear the cracks of the Métis fire and the shrill, repeated call of the *Northcote*'s distress whistle, but they were still too far away to go to her aid. The Canadians were just coming up on the outskirts of Batoche, when they came under fire from two houses overlooking the trail, just south of the church of St. Antoine. Middleton wasted no time on subtleties. He ordered his 9-pound cannon brought forward, and a few balls from these soon set one of the houses on fire. The handful of Métis stationed inside quickly abandoned the houses and retreated.

The way forward now clear, Middleton ordered a cautious advance again. They soon came upon the church of St. Antoine and its outlying rectory. Here, a new-fangled weapon was put into play. Before Middleton had left for the North-West, he had requested that the government purchase two Gatling guns. Minister of Militia and Defence Caron had wisely agreed to the request, and two of the weapons were quickly shipped up to Canada along with an American officer, Lieutenant A.L. Howard, who actually knew how to operate them. The Gatling gun was the forerunner of the modern machine gun, operated by a gunner who turned a crank that rotated a cylinder of barrels, the top centre of which was loaded with a bullet from a drum full of ammunition above it. Turning the crank fired bullets in rapid succession. The effects of the machine impressed Canadians and Métis alike, albeit in completely different ways.

Its debut could well have made a poor impression, however, as Lieutenant Howard brought his Gatling gun to bear on the church rectory. Unknown to him, the rectory housed priests, nuns and the families of refugees that Riel and Dumont had been keeping under house arrest, and as the bullets riddled walls and smashed windows, one of the priests flew a white sheet out of a window on the top floor. Luckily, someone noticed the white flag before the Gatling gun could do any damage to life or limb.

As the troops advanced past the church, however, they came under fire from the rifle pits ahead, and the scouts in the front dismounted and returned fire at their near-invisible enemy as best they could. Again, Middleton ordered his cannon brought forward. From the church they had a clear view down into Batoche, and they began to shell the most obvious and tempting targets, bombarding the buildings and tents in the small Métis hamlet. The shelling continued throughout much of the battle. The Métis soldiers were almost all forward in the rifle pits, but their women, children and other non-combatants were hiding

THE GATLING GUN.

The Gatling gun consists of a number of breach-loading rifled barrels revolving about a central shaft. These barrels are loaded and fired while revolving, and after each discharge the empty cartridge shells fall out. Each barrel is fired only once in a revolution of the gun, so that with each single revolution of the gun ten shots are fired, while the gun can revolve twice a second if need be. This would give a fire of 1200 shots per minute. The feeding of the gun is simple. A long tin box, called a feed case, holding a row of cartridges, is held by one man perpendicularly over a hopper at the breach of the gun, and cartridges fall in as they are wanted. Another man turns the crank by which the gun is revolved, and the firing goes on continuously. (sketch and caption in the *Winnipeg Sun,* 1885)

in the town. When the cannon shells thundered down on them, they fled in terror.

Middleton brought his infantry forward and began to position them across the trail. There followed a brief calm before the storm. Dumont could see that the Canadians had positioned their Gatling gun forward on their lightly defended left flank, just pass the church. Dumont quickly organized a group of Métis for a daring attempt to break through the Canadian lines and capture the Gatling gun. They crawled forward on their bellies under cover of some small aspen trees in a small gully just beyond the church, and when they were close enough, Dumont turned to his men.

"Let me go ahead," he said. "I have already been close enough to take a shot in the head." He grinned wildly at the men in his company.

He and his men shared a quick round of smiles, and then Dumont outlined his plan. "When I start shooting, we must take the bullet spitter and get down the trail as quickly as possible."

He planned to shoot the machine gun's operator and then rush up, grab the gun and take it back down the trail as his men covered him from the gully. With that, Dumont crept forward undetected and alone, the veteran plainsmen blending into the prairie he knew and loved so well.

"I was almost at the place where I could get a good shot away," he later recalled, "when my men began to fire." For the second time that day, the Métis had failed to execute Dumont's orders, and his plan was thwarted. The surprise was blown, and Middleton quickly sent reinforcements towards the Métis in the gully while pulling his Gatling gun and cannons back a little farther from the front. Dumont knew his plan had failed and withdrew.

Dumont then pulled his men around to the Canadian right, and the Métis attacked from the concealment of their rifle pits and whatever bushes and trees offered cover on the prairie. It was a bold move that threatened to outflank Middleton from his right side and cut off communications with his base camp, which had been established a little farther back. The fighting on the right intensified as the Métis attack pressed forward, moving from rifle pit to rifle pit. Alarmed, Middleton ordered Lieutenant Howard and his Gatling gun over to his imperilled right flank. It was this intimidating weapon, carelessly spitting lead over the battlefield, that checked the Métis hunters' advance.

Middleton then tried to counter, pushing his cannon forward on the trail in his centre and ordering them to shell the rifle pits. This action proved easier said than done because the Métis had cleverly concealed their rifle pits, and the gunners found themselves firing blindly into clumps of bushes. The Canadian soldiers did manage to place themselves in an exposed forward position, however, thus presenting excellent targets to the Métis. One of the gunners was killed, and a shocked Middleton again ordered his cannon to pull back.

That was when Dumont found an opportunity to try another plan. The wind was blowing towards the Canadians, and the prairie was fairly dry, so he and his men lit a prairie fire and watched as it burned towards the enemy. The main object was to destroy any potential cover that the Canadian troops could find on the prairie, but if he was lucky, Dumont knew he might send the Canadians into a panic as well. But the plan was checked abruptly when the wind shifted back towards the Métis lines, and the Canadians astutely back lit the prairie in front of them.

By this time, the campaign had stretched on for longer than any of the volunteers had anticipated. The Canadian troops were impatient to come to grips with their enemy but were frustrated by the elusiveness of their Métis foe and Middleton's seemingly over-cautious tactics. In Middleton's defence, he had received word from priests and Métis deserters who had come into his camp that the Métis were severely short of ammunition, so his caution was in some ways understandable because he

Unidentified fallen Métis at the Battle for Batoche

didn't want to lose lives unnecessarily. He reasoned that if he could first wear down the Métis, forcing them to expend their ammunition, he would suffer fewer casualties. On the other hand, the morale of his men was suffering. A war of attrition, requiring patience and professionalism in the combatants, was worst kind of fight for troops as untried as these Canadians.

So it was that late in the afternoon, Middleton met with his higher ranks to discuss whether to fall back to the previous day's camp or to make a more permanent encampment closer to Batoche. Continuing the battle into the evening was out of the question—Middleton had had enough for the day. The officers quickly agreed that a retreat all the way back to Dumont's Crossing would provide too many opportunities for the Métis to harass their troops. They decided instead to construct a base site for the entire army a few hundred yards from where the fighting had taken place. The Canadians unhappily began to withdraw.

The first day of the battle for Batoche was drawing to a close, and other than his 11 casualties, Middleton had little to show for his efforts.

CHAPTER EIGHT

The Battle for Batoche

For three days the fighting wore on, with a near constant stream of bullets and cannonballs descending on the Métis.

IT TURNED OUT THAT THE OFFICERS commanding the small Canadian army had chosen an unfortunate position to camp for the night. They were in the middle of a ploughed field situated in a small depression and ringed on several sides by clumps of bushes, which left them dreadfully exposed to pot shots from Métis snipers. As the last of the troops was making its way into the encampment, a group of Métis and Natives opened fire on the Canadians, wounding one soldier and killing two horses. Middleton rushed a group of men out to repulse the raid, but such occurrences continued throughout the night and, indeed, every night for the entire battle of Batoche. The Natives in Dumont's camp seemed to take a particular joy in these nightly guerrilla attacks.

But joy was in short supply among Dumont's men, who were so plagued with the drastic shortage of weapons and ammunition that they had to take extreme measures. A Native,

who was something of a gunsmith, patched up venerable muskets and shotguns as best he could, often just enough that they
might be pressed into service for a few more hours. A group of
Métis melted down old lead pots and kettles to case their own
bullets and shot. Dumont did even more, going on nightly for-
ays onto enemy ground, scavenging bullets left by Canadian
soldiers during that day's fighting and plucking rifles out of
dead men's hands. On those nights, bullets may as well have
been gold nuggets, so eagerly were they sought. Bonanza-like
excitement greeted the discovery of discarded ammo belts,
which contained up to 40 bullets each of the same calibre as
many of the Métis 12-shot hunting rifles.

Dumont directed the Métis efforts day and night with relentless will, the last man to retire from the nocturnal ammunition raids, the first man up in the morning to distribute the
guns and bullets collected the night before. He also made
another attempt to take out the Canadian's Gatling gun. On
the third day of fighting, Lieutenant Howard positioned the
weapon close enough to the Métis lines that Dumont thought
he might be able to sneak up and kill the gunner. In a virtual
repeat of what had happened in the previous attempt, the
anxious men who covered his approach fired too soon, spoil-
ing Dumont's chances at surprise. Lieutenant Howard spotted
Dumont entirely too close for comfort and opened fire on him.
In the next instant, Gabriel was facing the concentrated fire of
the revolving Gatling gun. Branches split and snapped all
around him as the deadly weapon spat its charges at him.
Dumont dug in under the lowest branches and waited, his life
hanging in the balance for crucial seconds. Only when
Howard stopped firing to let the gun cool was Dumont able
to retreat to the safety of the rifle pits.

For three nights, the probing raids continued; for three days
the fighting wore on, with a near-constant stream of bullets
and cannonballs descending on the Métis, who only returned

fire when a sure target presented itself. Throughout most of the battle, Louis Riel boldly strode from one rifle pit to the next, holding his crucifix to the sky and exhorting God to come to their aid. Dumont ran from pit to pit, offering encouragement and shouting orders, keeping a watch for Native reinforcements, but knowing in his heart that none would come. For three days, the air was thick with bullets and ordnance, but Métis casualties were astonishingly low. The Métis had set up dozens of dummies in their rifle pits to divert Canadian fire and lend the illusion of numbers. And while the dummies were riddled by rifle fire, only three Métis were wounded, and not a single death occurred among Dumont's men during the first three days of battle.

Nevertheless, scores of Métis deserted on the second night, even more on the third. No matter how strong Dumont's battlefield presence was, he couldn't get his men to forget the frightful odds they faced and their abysmal shortage of ammunition. For far too many, this last stand at Batoche began to look like suicide. And by the time the sun rose on May 12, the fourth day of fighting, Dumont's forces stood at barely 100 men.

> *"Force can succeed holding but no more—*
> *want more troops."*

The Canadians didn't know that they had been wasting their ammunition on dummies until the battle over, but they suspected that their passive commander was accomplishing little.

One trooper, Harold Rusden, later recalled, "General Middleton made a mistake when he thought that the men were settling down to their work and getting steadier. On the contrary, they were getting exasperated at the check and were getting dissatisfied and restless at this cold-blooded sort of fighting. They had no proof that they had killed a single rebel, and a soldier likes to see the fruits of his work the same as any other man.

They wanted to charge, and being young and inexperienced soldiers, could not understand why they should not charge."

Middleton was not about to do anything so rash. During the first three days of the battle, the major general confined his forces to cautious reconnaissance missions and probing attacks on the Métis positions around Batoche. His most successful efforts were directed at improving the entrenchment around the Canadian encampment slightly to the south of the Métis, which were effective in discouraging the night raids.

Middleton defended his tentative strategy. In his report about the campaign, he wrote that his cautious operations during the beginning of the battle were intended to steady his untried Canadian troops. He even stated that his day-to-day offensives weren't the actions of an indecisive and uncertain command, but a smaller part of an overarching strategy that relied on a gradual advance. Years after the Battle of Batoche, Middleton continued to state that everything had been under control, that all along, he had been confidently orchestrating the inevitable fall of Dumont's forces. Middleton's communications to Ottawa, however, belied such claims.

On May 11, what Middleton telegraphed Caron hardly read like a missive from a self-assured man.

"Am in rather ticklish position," Middleton wrote. "Force can succeed in holding but no more—want more troops."

Even with so little at their disposal, Dumont and his Métis had still succeeded in checking Middleton. In the end, the Métis were beaten, not by any of the Canadian army commander's plans, but by an act of disobedience.

"I have not received any orders to do what I am going to do."

On the morning of May 12, the fourth day of the battle, Lieutenant Colonel Arthur Williams of the Midland battalion assembled his troops. He addressed the ring of soldiers in a low voice, so that every man there had to strain to hear him.

"I have no orders to do what I am going to do," Williams said, "but Batoche can be taken and will be taken today. We will advance on the rifle pits in one sudden rush. I only ask that you follow me, and we will go as far as we can."

Colonel Williams, it is true, coveted the fame and political advantage that would be his if he became a war hero. But he was also acting on his military instincts, sensing the frustrated tension of his troops, who had been fighting for three full days without a single inch of progress.

On the evening of the third day, Colonel Williams secretly arranged with the colonels commanding two other battalions, Toronto's Royal Grenadiers and the 90th Winnipeg Rifles, to make a determined charge for Batoche, regardless of Middleton's plans. So on the afternoon of May 12, after another ineffectual probe by Middleton on the Métis left, Colonel Williams led his men forward on the Métis right, quietly at first. They moved forward through a small wooded gully a little past the church. A few surprised Métis spotted the soldiers, and scattered firing broke out along the Métis line. Dumont noticed the move and barked orders to his men, arranging them to counter what he was sure would be the last Canadian advance. Gabriel leapt into a rifle pit with 93-year-old Joseph Ouellette and began firing on Williams' Midlanders. Colonel Williams ordered his men to wait while the other two battalions moved up to cover their right flank. The Midlanders second advance was not silent, subtle or tentative. They charged out onto the plain with a great shout, leading with their bayonets.

The real fighting had begun. As the Canadians swept towards Batoche, the Métis waged a fighting withdrawal, running from rifle pit to rifle pit, firing as they fell back, contesting every inch of ground. As the Métis reached the last line of rifle pits, however, many of them simply ran out of

The last shots in the shelling of Batoche

ammunition. Métis fire slackened, the Canadians continued to push forward and the tide soon became unstoppable. As the Canadians swarmed around the last line of rifle pits, they shot the trapped Métis like fish in a barrel, and the majority of Métis casualties in the battle for Batoche occurred in these few minutes. Some of the elder Métis, such as Joseph Ouellette, made no attempt to escape. Hardened warriors of the old buffalo hunts, they had little desire to see the new West that was about to be imposed on their people and fought to the bitter end to prevent such a pass. Gabriel Dumont was standing next to Ouellette when Canadians rushed into their rifle pit and bayoneted the feisty old man. Dumont fought his way out and back to the town, where he prepared to make his last stand.

The Canadians rushed forward, past the dead and into the Métis village in confused, excited groups. Here their momentum stalled as they reached the relative safety of the buildings. But

Dumont had taken command of a group of six Métis and occupied a position in the woods overlooking the town. On his command, the men opened up on the militia below. They checked the Canadian advance completely, and for a time, the Canadians even feared the Métis might muster a counter-attack. But only seven men were in the woods—seven men against an army.

As Dumont and his six fought, a Métis named Daniel Ross came running up. Ross had been badly wounded while retreating from Batoche, but he managed to make his way out of town and towards the Métis on the rise. He collapsed on the ground before them, practically delirious from his wound.

"Gabriel!" he called out to his leader. "You are still alive!"

"Still, Daniel," Gabriel called out.

"I can't walk anymore," Ross said. "Lift me to a place where I can see the enemy. I have a few bullets left."

Touched by the man's bravery, Dumont looked away from his rifle site. "Are you dead or alive? That's a lot of blood you've lost."

"I won't last much longer," Ross answered.

"Then it is good to want to fight on," Dumont said. "You might get two deaths instead of one." Gabriel walked to where Ross was lying and dragged him out so that he could take more shots at the Canadians. By this time, Middleton's force had begun to push slowly forward again, and the pressure on the small group of Métis was becoming unbearable. The last pocket of resistance retreated into the woods, Dumont carrying the wounded Ross slung over his shoulder. Eventually, they found a tent occupied by the Tourond family a few miles from the fighting, where Dumont deposited his injured comrade.

The Métis put up a brave fight, but in the end, the Canadians' superior numbers and weaponry proved too great an obstacle to surmount. Almost all of the Métis casualties—12 men dead, three wounded—were suffered during the Canadians' last charge. By the time the dust settled over Batoche, Middleton's forces counted 10 more dead and 36 wounded.

Word of the fall of Batoche reverberated across the prairie, spreading quickly among the Native tribes and Métis settlements, killing any hope for reprisal against Ottawa and snuffing out the fighting spirit. A group of 60 well-armed Métis who had fought beside Chief Poundmaker at the Battle of Cut Knife Hill had heard Dumont's urgent call for help at the beginning of May. Riding hard for Batoche, they arrived on the morning of May 13, looking down into the Saskatchewan River valley to see the white flags flying from the buildings in Batoche. The dejected men turned back.

Rumours also persist that 100 Métis from the St. Albert area responded to the news of their people's victory at Fish Creek and set forth to aid the cause. They, too, turned back when advanced messengers returned with news of the total collapse of the Métis uprising at Batoche. Poundmaker, as well, decided to mobilize his Cree and come to Dumont and Riel's aid, but like the others, was too late.

"Don't worry, the enemy can't kill me."

Gabriel spent the rest of the day caring for his defeated followers. He found his wife Madeleine in the woods 600 yards from Batoche. She had set up a primitive field hospital, and with several other Métis wives, was tending to the men who had been wounded in defence of the village. It was also in the woods surrounding Batoche that he ran into his vaunted leader, Louis Riel, the only man he had deferred to during the course of the rebellion, the man who stood as the sole focus of Gabriel's Christian faith.

"What are we going to do?" Riel asked, looking pleadingly on the Métis general.

Gabriel had just witnessed the collapse of his people and had been dealt defeat for the first time in his life.

"We must die," he told Riel flatly. "You must have known that in taking up arms against such a power, we would be defeated."

But looking Louis in the face, Gabriel realized that Riel knew no such thing, that until the last moment, his leader was waiting for nothing less than divine intervention. When it didn't come, he was completely lost.

"I must go now, Louis," Gabriel said. "The women and children are facing a cold night in the woods. I have to go back to Batoche for food and blankets."

Riel blanched at the thought of Gabriel exposing himself to more danger. "Uncle, no. It's too dangerous."

Gabriel didn't look back as he strode away.

"Don't worry, the enemy can't kill me. Just stay close to the others. I'll see you later."

For the next few days Dumont remained consumed by the war, refusing to surrender, saturated in bitterness and hatred. He made three trips into Batoche, working throughout the night for the welfare of his people. Dumont crept back towards a tent on the outskirts of town where he thought some blankets might be stashed. By the light of the stars and moon, the experienced hunter could see a soldier standing guard by the entrance to the tent. A well-placed shot knocked the unfortunate man off his feet, and when the sound brought another man running, Dumont felled him too.

The stocky but lithe Métis was in and out of the tent in a the space of a heartbeat. He emerged with two blankets and two quilts, which he ran back to Madeleine's camp. Madeleine dealt with the crisis with her usual calm competence, working in concert with her husband to look after the band of refugees she had taken under her protective wing. Dumont's loyal bond to Louis Riel remained as strong as ever.

"Give these coverings to Madam Riel and her children this night," Gabriel said to Madeleine, handing her his first haul of stolen goods.

Most of the women and children hadn't eaten for the entire day, so Dumont's next priority was to find these hungry innocents some food. Recalling a Sioux lodge nearby, Dumont made it the target of his next foray. Running the whole way, he picked up a generous haul of dried meat. He then worked his way stealthily around Batoche and picked up a sack of flour before returning to Madeleine. And so Dumont returned to the Métis camp for the second time that night, sacks of the Sioux meat in one hand and a bag of flour slung over his shoulder.

"Divide this food among the women who have children," he said.

Gabriel then sought out Louis Riel, who was still in the camp. He walked in on a whispered conversation between Riel and his wife. He heard Riel saying "I hope God wants me to live."

Dumont cleared his throat and called a hushed greeting. Louis smiled to see Gabriel. "You are okay."

"Yes," Gabriel said. "I think it would be best if you flee, Louis. These hills will soon be crawling with Canadians. They will be looking for you. They will want your head."

Riel stood silently, looking as if he were fully aware of the historical importance of this moment.

"I will go back to Batoche and get you some horses," Gabriel continued. "And don't worry, you won't be the only one getting out of here. Everyone is anxious about what the Canadians are going to do tomorrow."

"What are you going to do?" Louis asked.

Gabriel smiled wearily. "I still have work to do." He did not know it at the time, but this would be the last time he saw Louis Riel.

Gabriel then returned to his wife.

"I'm going to go back to Batoche," he said to Madeleine. "Make sure that Louis and his family are looked after."

"Gabriel," Madeleine spoke. "The others have talked to me, they don't want to remain so close to Batoche. They are all afraid of what the Canadians might do if they capture us. There is talk of moving farther away."

"Let them go then," Gabriel said. "I only ask that you wait here for me. I need to go to back into Batoche one more time for horses."

"I will wait then," Madeleine said, "until you return."

Gabriel smiled, grateful for his wife's courage. "Don't worry about the Canadians," he said. "If the enemy captures you and blames you for my actions, tell them that you had nothing to do with my behaviour. Tell them that you had as much trouble managing me as they did."

The two shared a quiet laugh before Dumont again slipped into the night. Madeleine waited for her husband.

Dumont went on his third raid into occupied Batoche. Emmanuel Champagne told him that he had left his horses behind, so Dumont headed for the man's stables. For the most part, he had no problem evading the sentries positioned throughout town. But when he got to the stables, he discovered that a contingent of Mounties occupied it. A part of him longed to charge into the stables in a final blaze of glory and take down as many of the enemy as possible, so filled was he with the need for vengeance. But another part of him also wanted to return to his wife, and so he decided against the suicide mission. Returning to the camp, Dumont found his wife alone, and this time he moved her to a hiding place on a small island in the river. He set out again to capture some horses.

Dumont prowled through the dark, ever ready for an opportunity to continue the war. He had to acknowledge the defeat of his nation, but his warrior's heart refused a personal surrender. As he crept to Batoche, an object moving through a stand of trees caught his attention. Gabriel raised his rifle to his shoulder and took aim at the mysterious figure. His finger closed around the trigger, and he waited, poised to take down whoever emerged from the bush. When a Métis woman emerged carrying her daughter on her back, he dropped his weapon. He recognized Madame Vandal, whose husband had been killed in the defence of Batoche. Dumont could do little but point her in the direction of the other refugees and press forward.

Dumont continued on, collecting what he could and returning to his wife with a rather eclectic booty that included a goat, two mares, plates, pots, cutlery and a loaf of Canadian bread that he'd found on one of the trails. Madeleine had never ridden bareback, so Dumont walked on foot guiding her mount with a rope, while the second mare followed. She carried Dumont's quickly assembled provisions slung across her back. Thus, man and wife headed to the relative safety of the northeast edge of La Belle Prairie where they finally made camp for what little remained of the night.

Meanwhile, the Canadians in Batoche, stung by the mounting casualties that came with Gabriel's visits, promptly put out a warrant for both Métis leaders, Gabriel Dumont and Louis Riel. Mounties and soldiers combed the countryside for them, but Gabriel proved elusive. He seemed to be everywhere at once. Men reported seeing the stocky frontiersman running from a building on the outskirts of Batoche, a bag of flour hoisted over a shoulder. Hours later, Mounties were startled by the sight of a big bearded man darting among the trees with incredible speed, the silence of his movement through the woods incongruous with his bulk. Whenever he was spotted, he was always too far away, moving too fast for his pursuers to even come close to catching him. Although he was aware of the Canadian patrols, Dumont barely gave them a second thought, moving in and around Batoche with easy impunity.

Dumont with two of his friends, Napoleon Nault and M. Gladu, taken in 1890

"How is it that yesterday you fought against the police, and today you help them look for me?"

Dumont, dressed only in shirtsleeves, could not have slept well on the night of May 12, but he woke up with morning's first light. He ate a hurried breakfast, made sure Madeleine was well hidden and then went out to have a look at the situation in Batoche. What he saw made him wince. Every man, women and child who hadn't fled town had surrendered to the occupying Canadian force.

"I saw the houses at Batoche with white flags flying from the roofs," Gabriel later recalled. "I saw that everyone was surrendering. I learned that the group on the other shore, led by Napoleon Nault, had also given themselves up."

Nor did the shameful behaviour of the Canadian soldiers after the battle do anything to soothe Dumont's righteous anger. A reporter with the *Mail*, a Toronto newspaper, left an account of the pillaging:

> *What a distressing picture is offered by these Half-breed families, cruelly plundered and stripped by the volunteers. The soldiers only came out of the houses of the Half-breeds after having broken whatever they could not carry away; stoves, clocks, bedsteads, tables, etc., were all mercilessly destroyed by these raving maniacs. Poor mothers of families who had only one bed and one blanket were brutally deprived of these articles. The soldiers being unable to carry off the bed, took hold of the blanket, and splitting with their knives the ticking, which contained the feathers, enjoyed the sport of throwing them to the wind. The soldiers have robbed and destroyed everything they could lay their hands on in that region, leaving the residents in the most destitute condition.*

Gabriel moved around Batoche, soaking in the stories of his people and witnessing the handiwork of the troops with his own eyes. Putting aside his anger and accepting the loss of Batoche, Gabriel shifted his concentration to Louis Riel. Finding his friend and leader and getting him away from the Canadians became his chief concern. He employed all his tracking skills in this search, following the numerous trails that spread across the region, footprints that all fanned away from Batoche in panicked strides. He found nothing. He searched through the woods, creek bottoms and deserted camps. He found no trace of Louis Riel.

He searched among the fleeing families. And while he stumbled on sights that moved his heart—mothers sleeping under hay with their bawling infants, children who endured the cold night without any shoes on their feet—Riel was nowhere to be found. Dumont took the time to make some rawhide shoes for some of these children before resuming his search. Running into one group of refugees after another, Dumont asked everyone he met about Riel's whereabouts, but no one could give him any information.

He hunted for Riel for four days, despite his wife's urging to make his way for the safety of the American border. The countryside was saturated with posses looking for the outlawed Métis general, but Gabriel could not bring himself to leave without knowing what had happened to Riel. It became his obsession, even though the danger mounted daily.

One day, while Dumont was on the prowl, he spied a group of soldiers escorting three Natives. Dumont assumed that the Natives were prisoners, and without thinking, moved to liberate them. Creeping up on the group, his rifle at the ready, Gabriel was about to strike when the Natives spotted him, and to his surprise, shouted at the soldiers, warning them of his presence. The soldiers knew Dumont's reputation and, not too eager to confront a cornered bear, sent one of the Natives forward to parley. When the Native was close enough for the two men to speak, Dumont demanded that he halt.

"What's wrong, are you afraid of me?" the Native asked.

"Certainly," replied the disgusted Dumont. "How is it that yesterday you fought against the police, and today you help them look for me? I fear anything that looks like a man, but acts like a snake."

The Native took a few more steps towards Dumont. "Brother, you have no reason to fear me."

But Dumont stopped the man in his tracks, raising his Winchester to his shoulder and cocking the lever. "Don't come any closer or I will have to shoot you," he warned his erstwhile ally. He then sent the Native back with the following defiant message: "I will not lay down my arms—I will fight forever. And the first who comes for me, I will kill."

The three soldiers left with their skins intact, returning as quickly as they could with a large contingent of reinforcements. But by the time they got back, Dumont was nowhere to be found.

While the capture of Riel and Dumont had become Middleton's chief objective, it turned out to be a near-impossible task, especially where the formidable Dumont was concerned. When Middleton confronted Father André about the possible location of Gabriel Dumont, the priest snorted derisively.

"You are looking for Gabriel?" the priest scoffed. "You are wasting your time; there isn't a blade of grass on the prairie he does not know."

In the end, it turned out that the hunt for Dumont was far more hopeless than any of the hunters could have imagined. Gabriel was actually using the movements of the Canadian patrols against them, *tracking them* without their knowing. Thus, Dumont skilfully sought out their patrols, coolly following at a short distance and avoiding the path of their search.

"You will be looked upon as a silly fool."

On the third day after the Battle of Batoche, Gabriel sent Madeleine off to his father's home three miles from the occupied Métis town, telling her that he would see her later that evening. He secretly followed her the entire way to make sure she came to no harm and spent the rest of the day searching for Riel, who remained in hiding.

When he arrived at his father's home, he was greeted warmly, and father and son sat down to talk. Dumont began to unwind a little from the tension of the previous days and shared his plans with his father. Dumont was far from giving up the war; the bitterness of the Métis' defeat had curdled much of his better nature and judgement. He told his father that he intended to remain hiding out in the area for the rest of the summer, operating as a lone guerrilla, harassing the Canadian soldiers and police at every opportunity.

His father looked him straight in the eye and, with characteristic Dumont family forthrightness, told him just what he thought of the idea.

"I am proud you haven't given in," he told his son, "but if you go through with your idea of staying to kill people, you will be looked upon as a silly fool."

"Father—" Gabriel began in protest, only to be interrupted by the elder Isidore.

"Do you really want to make Madeleine a widow? Hasn't there been enough bloodshed? Why don't you listen to your wife and head for the border?"

These blunt words, coming from Gabriel's venerable father, struck the Métis warrior deep. The younger Dumont saw their undeniable wisdom.

"I have always taken your advice before," he told his father, "and I want very much to follow it again." Dumont still felt that he couldn't abandon his chief, however, and he added, "I will leave if I cannot find Riel."

His father then told him that Gabriel's brother-in-law, Moïse Ouellette, held a letter from Middleton that was addressed to Riel and Dumont. The news that a family member had been corresponding with the enemy instantly set Dumont's blood boiling, and it was all he could do to keep his calm veneer intact in front of his father. Muttering to himself in rage as soon as he closed his father's door behind him, Dumont set off to visit Ouellette.

When confronted, Ouellette became defensive and claimed that the letter only offered the two Métis leaders justice.

"Go to the devil!" was Dumont's terse reply. "The government has skinned you like sheep. It has taken your arms from you so that all you are able to do is what you're told."

Gabriel spat at his brother-in-law's feet and was seriously considering striking the man.

"Yes, it would be a great thing for every man along the river to keep fighting, even to the death, but some of us have families to think about. Some of us have children." Ouellette was trying to remain calm, but his voice shook with emotion.

Dumont reined in his anger, reminding himself that the man standing in front of him was family.

"You tell Middleton," he said, jabbing Ouellette's chest, "that I am in the woods and that I still have 90 cartridges left. He and his men are welcome to come and get me."

Before Ouellette could say a word, Gabriel spun on his heel and strode away.

But as much as Gabriel would have liked this exchange with his brother-in-law to be his last, he realized later that Ouellette may have had some contact with Louis, given that he was commissioned to deliver Middleton's message to both Riel and himself. Dumont returned to visit his brother-in-law early the next day, May 15. What Ouellette told him froze the blood in Gabriel's veins and killed what was left of his will to fight. Ouellette informed him that he had already found Riel and delivered the letter.

"I'm sorry, brother," Moïse said, "but unlike yourself, Riel is a man of reason. He went immediately to surrender to the English general."

The news struck Dumont like a hammer. He looked out past Ouellette and onto the beloved prairie he had always called home. It looked to him then like a crumbling kingdom. The remnant of the rebellion that Dumont had fiercely clung to in the dark days after the fall of Batoche had slipped through his fingers, and the hardened Métis warrior had been powerless to stop it. He knew that his course of action was clear now. He was the only one left. It was time to head south to the safety of the United States.

CHAPTER NINE

Show Business

"We set out by the grace of God."

GABRIEL DUMONT RESOLVED TO head south. He spent the night of May 15 camped with a few hunters who still hadn't given up the fight. He gave these men the bitter news, and they passed the night in sombre silence, gathered around the fire contemplating their defeat. His mind made up, Dumont was anxious to leave. The next morning, he hastily threw together supplies for the long and dangerous journey. He saddled his favourite horse, gathered all the ammunition he could find, packed up *Le Petit* and strapped a revolver around his waist.

While he was preparing, he asked his favourite nephew, Alexis Dumont, to run two specific errands. First, Alexis rode out to where Madeleine was camped and told her that her husband was leaving for the United States. Relieved that Gabriel was finally burying the hatchet and making for safety, Madeleine sent young Alexis away with her blessings.

"Tell him that my prayers are with him," Madeleine said, "and I will follow him soon."

Alexis then paid a visit to Gabriel's father and told him that Gabriel was in for a long journey and could use any food the old man could spare. Unfortunately, he didn't have much at all; the senior Dumont's cupboards were all but bare in the difficult days following the rebellion. All that Isidore could spare were six *galettes*—thick unleavened bread much like bannock. Each cake weighed about three-quarters of a pound, and they were the only provisions Dumont would have for his 600-mile journey. The trusted nephew then made his way back to Gabriel and delivered the *galettes* along with Madeleine's parting wishes.

Word of Gabriel's departure spread like telegraph pulses through the Métis grapevine, and a small group of young hunters rode out to witness their leader's departure. None of the typical Métis boisterousness characterized the hasty farewell party—words were heartfelt, but brief and saturated with sadness. Dumont vaulted onto his courser and wheeled the steed about as he gave a final wave. He had gone only about 100 yards when he heard a voice calling to him. Gabriel reined in his horse and turned to see one of the Métis galloping towards him. It was Michel Dumas, a young man famous for his outsized sense of humour and flamboyance. Dumas pulled his horse up beside Gabriel's.

"Monsieur Dumont," Michel said with a wide grin on his face, "the thought of my leader making such a long trip without a guard is appalling to me. I humbly offer my services."

Dumont smiled. "Are you armed?"

"I have this Hudson's Bay musket," Dumas said, pulling an antiquated rifle from his horse's saddle. "Unfortunately, it does not work, and I have no powder, shot or ammunition of any kind."

"Well then, do you have any food?"

Michel Dumas (c1849–1901), one of the leaders in the 1885
North-West Rebellion, who fled south with Dumont

"That I do," answered Dumas. "There are a few *galettes* in
my saddlebags."

Gabriel stared at the beaming Dumas for a moment before
breaking into a roaring fit of laughter.

"Your company will be welcome, Michel. Let us depart."

And the two Métis fighters set off together heading south,
the sound of their laughter carrying to the huddle of Métis

hunters who waited until they were two specks on the horizon before returning to their homes.

Dumont continued with the same tactics of evasion that proved so successful after the fall of Batoche. The two carefully followed the Canadian patrols as they made their way south. With their skill, cunning and knowledge of the country, the pair managed to completely evade the soldiers and police. They may have been aided by the Métis leader's fierce reputation because many of the Canadians on the hunt were somewhat reluctant to be the ones to find the armed and angry Gabriel Dumont. More than one patrol conveniently ignored the tracks of two riders because it may have led to confrontation.

Dumont planned a 600-mile journey when the U.S. border actually lay only 300 miles away. The indirect route was largely dictated by terrain because Gabriel sought out natural cover and kept his distance from larger settlements, forts and Hudson's Bay Company posts. As well, the pace at which they were travelling did not allow for much hunting and trapping along the way, and so he found himself going on lengthy detours to obtain food and supplies from Natives and Métis who owed him favours. Gabriel had friends all across the Plains, and as he and Michel made their way south, scores of families opened their doors. Yet, despite the aid extended to the two fugitives, it was far from an easy journey, and the two men often suffered through long days of cold and hunger. It was during these hard periods that Dumont thought of Louis Riel. He thought of Louis Riel, and he prayed, supplicating to the Virgin Mary for help and guidance.

"At least we don't have to sleep outside."

After 11 tense days, Dumont and Dumas made it to the American border, where they both knelt to say the rosary in gratitude. Just outside Fort Assiniboine, the two turned themselves in to the first American military personnel they came across. Dumont did not mince words. He told the commanding officer of the patrol, Sergeant Prévost, exactly who he was and why he was in the United States. The Métis rebellion had captured the attention of most of the continent on both sides of the border. Newspapers from coast to coast covered the unfolding drama, and Prévost was well informed of what was going on up North, so did not need any elucidation of Dumont's story.

The nervous sergeant escorted the pair back to the fort and locked them in a jail cell, while he relayed the exciting news to his superior. As the door of the two Métis' jail cell slammed shut behind them, Dumont took in the bleak accommodations and let out one of his trademark bursts of laughter.

"Well, Michel, it seems that the Americans are just as happy to have us as guests as the Canadians," Dumont said.

"Such luxury," Michel said. "I wonder if Monsieur Macdonald's holding pens compare."

Dumont sat heavily on one of the beds. "This will be just fine. At least we don't have to sleep outside tonight."

The fort's commander had no idea what to do with such an illustrious prisoner, but he was sure that the decision rested on greater shoulders than his. Telegram begat telegram, and eventually, the news reached Washington, where President Grover Cleveland sat down with his secretaries of state and war to decide what to do about the sensitive matter.

It took Cleveland and his advisors two days to give the order to set Dumont free from military arrest. The American executive did, however, leave their options open to civil action if the Canadian and British government should apply diplomatic pressure to extradite the former general of the North-West Rebellion. Meanwhile, the fort's commander directed Sergeant Prévost to the stockade and ordered him to find more comfortable accommodations for his famous prisoner. Now that

Dumont was a free man, the sergeant allowed himself to be in awe of the frontier legend. Prévost stammered an apology for locking the two men in a cell, muttering something about mistakes and injustice, which neither Gabriel nor Michel could make out. He then promptly led the two Métis into one of the best rooms in the fort.

The Americans at Fort Assiniboine were genuinely sorry for placing such a celebrity in prison, and after his initial incarceration, Dumont was given the best treatment to be found in a frontier fort. Indeed, Gabriel Dumont had never been so fawned over in his entire life. They had an officer waiting on them throughout the day and were given the best food in the larders. Star-struck American soldiers lined up to see Gabriel. Most men just stood and gawked, but if they spoke French or Sioux, they would prod the Métis warrior for tales of his adventures. Dumont, always the gregarious story-teller, was happy to oblige.

"He is trying to save me from this box."

Dumont and Dumas walked out of Fort Assiniboine as free men on May 29, while Riel was in Regina, languishing in the confines of a Canadian jail. On July 6, a formal charge of treason was brought against the Métis leader, and two weeks later, on July 20, his historic trial began. The trial did not appear to offer much hope for Riel. Louis' cousin, Charles Nolin, who was involved in the early stages of the 1885 Rebellion, only to desert the Métis cause after things became violent, offered damning testimony against the accused. And while Riel fought to defend himself and the actions of his people by claiming that the Métis were only defending their rights, Riel's attorneys insisted on using an insanity defence. The trial was, to say the least, hard on the erstwhile Métis saviour. In his final speech, Riel's thoughts turned to the man he had affectionately called Uncle.

"Is Gabriel Dumont inactive?" he asked of the courtroom with a typical Riel rhetorical flourish. "I believe not. He is trying to save me from this box."

In this case, Riel's prophetic musings were somewhere near the mark. Dumont was actually concocting a plan to rescue his imperilled friend. After his release from custody, Gabriel made the rounds of the Métis communities in Montana, contacting old friends and relations. He talked to newspapermen about the sorry circumstances of the man he thought of as his chief. He tried to make it seem as if Riel had always been for peace, and that it was Dumont that had pushed for violence. Many in Montana were not well disposed towards the Canadian authorities, and Riel was fondly remembered by those who had dealt with him while he lived in that state. Positively received among the Americans, Gabriel began to earnestly scheme on a plan for Riel's liberation.

Other northern desperadoes from the rebellion trickled into Montana, including Gabriel's brother Edouard. They sought out their former commander and eagerly supported his plan. Gabriel's movement to free Riel seemed to be picking up steam, as more and more men donated time and resources. Dumont travelled far and wide across Montana, venturing into Indian country along the border with Canada, establishing contacts, accepting recruits and securing funds. He suffered some setbacks, one in particular that strained his friendship with Michel Dumas, whose irrepressible *joie de vive* sent him on a drinking binge with Gabriel's rescue money.

It was no time to indulge in resentment, however. After that embarrassing setback, Dumont redoubled his efforts and made his drastically reduced funds stretch as far as they could for his daring scheme. Dumont planned to slip across the border with a small group of his most committed and able men, travelling stealthily up to Regina, where they would stage a lightning quick raid at night and free Louis. Dumont and his men could then spirit Riel to the border and beyond to safety. Dumont arranged way stations along the route back from Regina where the raiding party could rapidly get fresh horses or any needed provisions and quickly continue on their ride to freedom. If successful, this would make for a legendary "hunting" story indeed.

Meanwhile, the Riel's situation had become dire. The jury in Regina had convicted him of treason. Riel's trial was rapidly becoming a divisive issue that aggravated the differences the young Dominion's two major camps—French Roman Catholic and English Protestant. The English Protestant elements in Ontario, still harbouring a lust for revenge over the 1870 murder of Thomas Scott, would settle for nothing less than Riel at the end of a rope. The French were much more sympathetic to Riel, whom they considered a part of their beleaguered North American family.

As for Macdonald, caught between a rock and a hard place, the controversy had already persuaded the wily John A. not to pursue extradition of Dumont from the United States—a sleeping dog he was quite happy to let lie. In addition, pressure from Québec caused the prime minister and his government, under protest from Ontario, to delay Riel's execution so that the much-questioned sanity of the accused might be investigated. Riel had refused a defence of insanity during the trial, and a panel of three examining physicians, albeit with one dissenting opinion, pronounced the infamous Métis sane. On the basis of this official report, the federal Cabinet sentenced Riel to hang.

Time was running out, and Dumont needed to act. Unfortunately a problem was developing. Although Riel's would-be rescuers, tried to keep their plans secret, an operation as broad and bold in scope as theirs was simply impossible to keep

Louis Riel facing the court during his trial in 1885

under wraps, and rumours of Dumont's planned rescue buzzed across the prairies like mosquitoes after an early summer wet spell. The rumours brought anxious controversy and suspicion. Toronto newspapers speculated that the Macdonald Conservatives were actually planning to allow Riel's rescue as a desperate way out of the French-English conflict, which threatened to crush the government.

The government did not treat the rumours lightly, especially because they involved Gabriel Dumont, whose skills in such matters were well known after the three battles of the 1885 Rebellion. The government doubled the guard around Riel: three troops (300 men) of the North-West Mounted Police were kept in Regina, forming layers of armed men around the condemned. With a small army as his personal guard, Riel was now untouchable. Dumont's spies in Regina sent word of the heightened security around Louis Riel, and the former Métis general was forced to acknowledge that what had been an extremely risky venture had now become a futile one.

Dumont could do nothing more than wait and hope that a chink in the defences around Riel might present itself, but one never did. On November 16, 1885, Louis David Riel dropped from the prepared wooden scaffolding in Regina until the rope around his neck broke the fall, leaving his lifeless body dangling above the prairie of his birth. Riel's body was laid to rest in St. Boniface where he had been educated as a young man.

"I never really knew her."

Thus, the rudder that had guided the course of Dumont's life for the past year vanished, and Dumont found himself adrift in strange waters. The arrival of his loyal wife Madeleine, who had managed to persuade her brother-in-law Patrice Fleury to escort her to Montana so that she could be reunited with her husband, provided a rare respite of joy. But Madeleine, too, carried sadness with her. She informed her husband that his father had just passed away. The former Métis leader, who had witnessed the defeat of his people, the death of one son, Isidore, and the banishment of another, Gabriel, found himself unable to carry the weight of his years any longer and silently gave up the ghost.

Madeleine also seemed much weaker when she and Gabriel reunited. She looked pale and thin and was prone to long coughing spells. Dumont repeatedly asked his wife if she was ill, but the stoic frontier woman steadfastly maintained nothing was wrong, her inbred work ethic not allowing her a word of complaint. Madeleine was likely suffering from tuberculo-sis, yet she did not allow the disease to impede her utility, and she continued to help her husband any way she could in their new home. A few months later, in the spring of 1886, she fell from a carriage and never fully recovered, unable even to stand on her two feet for longer than a few minutes at a time. A few weeks later, she died.

In his later years, Dumont reflected on his wife. "I never really knew her," he said, sadly. Theirs had been a relationship forged and tested in a harsh world as yet untouched by romantic notions of true love. The two had depended upon one another for survival, a relationship that had bred a deep, mutual respect and sturdy loyalty. The two had relied on each other, been companions and over the years a strong bond of love developed between them. Her passing was a hard blow for Gabriel Dumont.

Dumont's health, too, remained less than perfect for some time. The after effects of the near-fatal wound he received while fighting at Duck Lake continued to bother him. Shortly after his arrival in the United States, the gash reopened, forcing the hardy Dumont to submit to the attentions of a doctor.

"When I coughed hard it was like being hit over the head with a hammer, and many times I lost consciousness and fell," Dumont recalled. "One day in a blacksmith's shop I fell face first on top of a pile of angle iron and marked up my whole face."

This accident in particular seems to have alarmed Dumont, who was unused to and uneasy at the thought of being left so defenceless. Luckily, the blackout episodes eased as Gabriel slowly recovered.

In the meantime, Dumont needed to make a living. The Métis leader had been rendered nearly penniless by the failed rebellion. Buffalo were even scarcer in Montana than in Canada, and it was difficult indeed for a hunter—even of

Dumont's skill—to support himself with his trade. Neither did Gabriel possess the knowledge of the local terrain to act as a guide, nor the capital to set up business as a trader—the two other occupations with which he was most familiar. Living in Lewiston, Montana, with his brothers, the charismatic Gabriel made many friends, but there was little worthwhile farmland in the area, and so the three brothers talked of moving their families farther east to the Turtle Mountains. In the end, Dumont decided against the move, not at all enthusiastic about the plodding, patient life of the farmer.

In the summer of 1885, Gabriel was still scheming to break Louis out of prison, when an exotic opportunity presented itself shortly after Michel Dumas' drinking binge consumed the money saved for Riel's rescue. Major John Burke, the general manager of Buffalo Bill Cody's famous Wild West Show, arrived in Montana. Burke sought out the renowned Métis warrior, hoping to tempt Gabriel into signing up as one of the show's stars. But Dumont, too engrossed with his ongoing plans to rescue Riel, had politely refused. Dumas, however, jumped at the opportunity to get himself away from the mess he'd had made of his reputation in the area, and eagerly took Burke up on his offer. Dumas headed east to join the show, while Dumont continued in his efforts to rescue his friend.

But Dumont had kept his options open, telling Burke that he might reconsider at a later date. So when Burke delivered Cody's offer again the following summer, Dumont had ample reason to reconsider. He was broke; both his wife and Riel were dead; and the prospects for a settled life in Montana seemed bleak. Dumont also reasoned that exposure in Buffalo Bill's show might further the Métis cause. So it was that in June 1886, Gabriel Dumont boarded a train for the first time in his life and headed for Philadelphia to join Buffalo Bill Cody's famous Wild West Show, beginning a chapter of his life incredibly different from anything he had hitherto known.

"Ladies and Gentlemen, I give you Gabriel Dumont, the Half-breed general!"

On June 7, a wide-eyed Gabriel Dumont rolled into the city of brotherly love and was met at the train station by an enthusiastic Bill Cody.

"So!" Cody exclaimed. "This is the famous Gabriel Dumont. Welcome to Buffalo Bill's Wild West Show!"

The two exchanged a handshake, and Dumont, speaking through an interpreter, returned his fellow plainsmen's greetings with equal admiration. Cody had also been a buffalo hunter of remarkable courage and skill. Dumont knew it, and beneath the fancy clothes and the showman's exterior, he sensed a man used to the split-second decisions of life and death.

William Frederick Cody, or Buffalo Bill, as he became more commonly known throughout North America and Europe, spent most of his youth on the American frontier. There, he amassed an impressive adventurer's resume, spending time as a Pony Express rider, Native scout, occasional horse thief and buffalo hunter. Cody had already developed a reputation among those who knew the West when, in 1873, a writer named Ned Buntline persuaded Cody to feature in one of the sensational dime novels Buntline was famous for. Thanks to Buntline's prodigious talents for lies and exaggeration, Cody became a living legend among the legions of eastern American readers who were fascinated with their feral frontier.

In 1883, Cody capitalized on his fame by organizing his famous Wild West Show. Eastern audiences, hungry with nostalgia for the old West they had played their part in destroying, flocked to see sensational displays of western legends doing what they did best. In stages and under pavilions, actors driving stagecoaches were subjected to mock hold-ups by bands of ruthless desperadoes, or murdered by tribes of howling Natives. Battles such as the Little Big Horn were colourfully

Buffalo Bill Cody, in front of a Wild West Show wagon

re-enacted for the crowds. Women sharpshooters such as Annie Oakley entertained easterners with impressive displays of coolness and skill.

The show's fame grew so much that it eventually went on two tours throughout Europe. Dumont participated in neither, although he was rumoured to have gone on the second tour to France. In his later years, the senior Métis dismissed the tale, revealing with an irrepressible grin, that the indefatigable rogue, Michel Dumas, had impersonated him on the tour through France—before being unceremoniously fired for his wayward love of wine, women and song.

After Cody and Dumont met in the train station, Nate Salisbury, the show's co-proprietor, joined Dumont in the carriage ride to his tent at Philadelphia's Gentleman's Driving

Park, which had been leased for the Wild West Show's two-week run in the Pennsylvanian city. That carriage ride must have been awe-inspiring for a man who had never before seen a city larger than Winnipeg. Perhaps he also began to understand the forces that had been arrayed against his and Riel's rebellion. Of course, he had heard of the bigger eastern cities, but witnessing their size and teeming streets firsthand was something else entirely.

Gabriel's name adorned billboards, and a short biography of his life was printed in Buffalo Bill's publicity handbook. Burke showed the Métis hunter the write-up, but the illiterate Dumont looked at the booklet and shrugged, unimpressed by the unintelligible print. The following day marked the start of Gabriel Dumont's career in show business. For a man who had spent his life employing all of his skills, smarts and resources to survive, this must have seemed very strange "work" indeed. On his first day, he was featured with an assortment of other western characters in the show's main opening parade, which circled a huge tent in front of a cheering audience.

Another part of his act had him sitting in front of his tent with *Le Petit* resting across his knees and a scowl on his face. This must have seemed more than a bit ridiculous to a man who had led a small army into battle. But having written his mark on the contract Buffalo Bill presented him, Gabriel stuck with the show. Dumont eventually learned to enjoy the frightened and excited reactions of the crowds. He still loved to tell his stories, and he made sure that his interpreter was on hand when the braver souls among the crowd came down to ask him about his adventures in the North-West.

Dumont, like the famous Annie Oakley, was also employed as a sharpshooter. The show's announcer, Frank Richmond, introduced Dumont thus: "And now, ladies and gentlemen, from the faraway plains of Canada, we bring you the one, the only, the incomparable Gabriel Dumont! The man who, with a handful of followers, defeated a vastly superior Canadian army twice, before himself giving way in the face of overwhelming odds. The man who rode 800 miles through dust, flood and fire to elude nearly 2000 Canadian army police scouts who were sent out to capture him and who finally reached the blessed sanctuary of the United States of America! Ladies and Gentlemen, I give you Gabriel Dumont, the Half-breed general!"

Such sensationalism was typical of Cody and Salisbury's promotion of their stars, and the grizzled Métis did his best not to disappoint. He charged out wildly across the exhibition field, reigning in his mount just before the edge of the field and dashed back to the centre of the pavilion just as four blue glass balls were thrown into the air. Dumont then loosed *Le Petit* from its scabbard and brought his old rifle into action, shattering all four balls in quick succession with four cracks from his rifle. By the time Dumont drove his rifle back into its holster, the crowd was on its feet, whistling and applauding his impressive feat of horsemanship and marksmanship.

It must have all seemed surreal to Dumont. He wandered around Buffalo Bill's camp and met some of the other performers—cowboys, sharpshooters and Mexican rough riders. Dumont met and tried to talk with Cheyenne and Pawnee from the south, but the language barrier proved impossible.

Dumont was excited to learn that a group of Sioux was performing with Buffalo Bill's show, and he went to meet them. Chief American Horse greeted Dumont as warmly as a lost brother. The Sioux, of course, had known of and respected Dumont for years, but his role in the recent rebellion against the white man had truly made him a hero in their eyes.

The Sioux held an impromptu feast and party to welcome the famous Métis rebel. They passed around a pipe, and Bill Cody, with a good sense for publicity, quickly rounded up any and all available journalists to report the event for the next day's newspapers. The feast proved to be such a media coup that Cody began staging the event at other shows in other cities. Dumont didn't mind; he was happy to find an island of familiarity amid this strange eastern urban sea.

The troupe continued to perform, and eventually, the show moved on to New York City. Rumours had been circulating that the Canadian government intended to grant a general amnesty to all those involved in the North-West Rebellion, but Dumont, who certainly had grounds to doubt the Canadian English, didn't get his hopes up, that is, until the morning of July 22, 1886. Dumont was preparing his saddle, horse and rifle for another day of work, when he was interrupted by the sound of a whooping crowd. Bill Cody led a band of excited Sioux to Dumont's tent.

"Have you heard the good news, Gabriel?" Cody shouted to him above the noise. "The Canadian government has proclaimed an official amnesty. You are free to go back home."

His interpreter translated Cody's words, and Dumont stood in silent shock, trying to digest the information. The Sioux pressed in around him, clapping him on the back. Some say that at that moment, Dumont turned to wipe away tears. If he did, then that would have been the only time anyone saw the vaunted Métis fighter cry. He'd feared that he might never live to see the day when the home he loved, the land for which he had fought, lay open to him again. And although the 1885 rebellion—the pivotal event of his life—would always send echoes through his remaining years, the war was finally over. After barely two months with the Wild West Show, the road home was open.

"To my own people I will tell of the fighting.'

His Sioux friends threw him an impromptu party to celebrate the good news, and Bill Cody was gracious enough to offer

Dumont a release from his contract. But Dumont was impressed with the almost brotherly way Cody had treated him. He also viewed the contract as seriously as the treaties he had once negotiated or any other promise he made in his life. So Gabriel declined Cody's generous offer and decided to complete his tenure.

That summer, while he was performing in New York, Dumont ran into a few characters from his past. He was resting after a show one evening, when Lieutenant Howard, the American officer who had manned the Gatling gun at Batoche, walked into his tent. Howard had gone to the Wild West Show that night hoping to have a conversation with the legend he had faced down the barrel of a gun.

"Greetings Mr. Dumont," an obviously nervous Howard introduced himself through an interpreter. "I fought against you. I was a gunner at Batoche."

Dumont stared at his former opponent in silence, remembering the harrowing moments he lay in the copse of trees as the Gatling gun rained bullets all around him.

"But that's all over," Howard continued. "I am no longer against you. Even then I never shot at you, I only fired in the air, just to scare you. That's what I was hired for."

Dumont appreciated being lied to about as much as he enjoyed Howard's insinuation that the Gatling gun had frightened him. Dumont did not even look at Howard when he gave his gruff response.

"I tried hard to kill you."

Before Dumont was officially pardoned, Leif Crozier sought him out. One might suspect Dumont of harbouring a grudge against the man who had ordered the volley that killed his brother, Isidore. But Gabriel was a man who had grown up in the rough and tumble world of men west of the 100th meridian, where men might brawl one day and then count on each other for their lives the next.

Dumont could certainly hold grudges, but these were always directed at more abstract bodies. For example, he could never seemed to forgive the Roman Catholic priesthood for its opposition to the Métis during the rebellion. For real, flesh and blood people that had been a part of his life, Dumont seemed to possess an extraordinary capacity of forgiveness. He even resumed his friendship with Charles Nolin, the man who had deserted after the battle of Duck Lake and offered such damaging testimony against Louis Riel.

The meeting between Crozier and Dumont was actually quite friendly. In a way, Crozier served as a kind of reminder of Dumont's dearer days along the South Saskatchewan, and so he was genuinely happy to see the Mountie in the teeming anonymity of New York City. They shook hands.

"What are you doing here in New York City?" Dumont asked with a broad grin. "And without your police uniform on either."

Crozier told Gabriel that he had left the service and was returning to his native Ireland. His layover in New York coincided with Buffalo Bill's performance, and when he noticed that Dumont was to be one of the stars, he felt compelled to see the man whom he had once faced across a battlefield.

"I must say," Crozier continued, "your show was incredible. I don't feel so bad about losing to you and your men if the rest of the Métis were half the marksmen you are."

Gabriel smiled at the compliment. "You're lucky we didn't have more bullets to give you or it could have been much worse."

Crozier asked Dumont how he was enjoying his celebrity status, but Dumont was already someplace else, lost in thoughts of Duck Lake and the land and people he missed so much. If Dumont was enjoying the strange sights and sounds of his urban adventure, Crozier's presence reminded him of a past now gone forever. Noticing the shift in Dumont's expression,

Crozier hastily bid Dumont farewell and wished him the best of luck with his impending amnesty. Gabriel was sad to see him go.

Dumont continued to work in the Wild West Show until the fall of 1886, but after the Canadian government divested him of his outlaw status, interest in the Métis warrior began to decline. As an outlaw rebel on the run from the Canadian government, he commanded some notoriety, but after the general amnesty, the fickle focus of public curiosity slipped away from Gabriel.

One witty eastern reporter noted, "Gabriel Dumont studied the big crowds more than they studied him."

It was time to move on, and while Dumont returned intermittently to work for Buffalo Bill's extravaganza over the next two years, it would never again be in the role as one of the show's stars. Dumont joined the equivalent of the show's chorus and played his small part in mock hold-ups and shootouts to earn some money.

Even while his first period of employment with Wild Bill was drawing to a close, Dumont received word that another audience was interested in hiring him to speak about Louis Riel and the rebellion they had brought about. Dumont was initially suspicious, but when he learned that it was a French Canadian community in Holyoke, Massachusetts, Gabriel warmed to the idea.

"To the English, I will not talk," Gabriel said to one of his Sioux friends on the Wild West cast, "but to my own people, I will speak of the fighting."

So it was that Dumont was briefly engaged as a public speaker. His speech was unadorned but honest as he spoke to eager audiences numbering in the hundreds about the dramatic sweep of events that had embroiled the North-West in violence and bloodshed from 1884 to 1885. Dumont's lectures were warmly received: one appreciative community awarded him a gold watch and chain and another presented him with a silver medal.

Gabriel was pleased, even touched at the response, but the life of a public speaker was not for him either. He returned west to visit friends and relatives in Montana and Dakota for a time, but Dumont's life was unsettled and shifting. He returned again to the East where his contacts among the French Canadians brought him into brief contact with President Grover Cleveland, who was also interested in meeting the famous Canadian rebel.

During the winter of 1887–88, his eastern contacts again provided Gabriel with a new direction in life. With the help of Monsieur Riboulet, a Staten Island cork merchant, Dumont began a correspondence with his former comrade-in-arms, Maxime Lépine, as well as some of the most prominent nationalist political figures in Québec. Through Lépine, Dumont learned of the sorry state of the Saskatchewan Métis, many of whom were still living practically destitute, having yet to receive the land promised them by the Canadian government. Dumont complained to the government and pushed for action.

The renewed connection with his home reinvigorated Dumont's enduring concern for his people as well as his anger against the clumsy giant of Ottawa. He even remarked to Father Albert Lacombe that, although he was committed to more peaceful means, knowing that they would better advance the Métis' interests, he felt like taking up arms again. While no such thing happened, Gabriel thought of continuing the fight in another way, as he considered having someone transcribe the story of his life.

"I shall recount the mode of life and the custom of Natives and Half-breeds and also the truth of the rebellion in the North-West in 1885," he said to a visiting Bishop Taschereau in 1888. "I wish to tell the truth about my friend and chief Louis David Riel, also my life since that time. My tale will render a service to

Gabriel Dumont with Madame Riboulet, whose husband helped Dumont tell his story to a Québec Member of Parliament

the Half-breeds and do homage to truth, so that everyone will know how and why we fought." As he grew older, Gabriel grew more and more concerned about the opinion of posterity.

At the same time, Dumont hoped for some personal justice. His home, after all, had been looted of its most prized possessions and burned to the ground by Middleton's advancing army. He had fled the country with little more than his horse and rifle and was still only living one step above destitution.

"There is power in my story, thunder in my voice," Gabriel told the bishop. "For I have fought the just fight and lost everything in defence of my people's rights."

Recognizing how dangerous Gabriel's story might be to the peace and order of Canada, Taschereau tried to dissuade Dumont. But Gabriel would not be discouraged. With the help of Monsieur Riboulet, he wrote to the Québec Member of Parliament R. Préfontaine. He asked Préfontaine to pass along a threat to the government: if nothing was done, Gabriel warned, he would give public lectures in Québec and possibly in France on the grave injustices suffered still by the Métis. Some political forces in Québec eagerly anticipated the arrival of Gabriel Dumont and his angry politics.

Nationalists opposed to the Macdonald hierarchy in Ottawa had gained power in Québec in 1887. They owed their office largely to the execution of Louis Riel and the simmering feelings of discontent left over from the 1885 rebellion. The nationalists hoped to consolidate their position by making political hay out of Dumont's offer. Here, they thought, was a living example of a victim of the tyranny of English Canada that they might parade before their constituents.

Dumont responded enthusiastically when these politicians invited him on a speaking tour of Québec.

"Riel is dead, and I am anxious to speak for him in the name of those for whom he laid down his life," Dumont wrote to Laurent Olivier David, a newspaper editor and member of the Québec Legislative Assembly, "…and no matter if I should have to die after delivering simply one lecture that would not debar me from going among you."

So it was that in the spring of 1888, Dumont travelled to Montréal, the same city that his grandfather had set forth from on his journey to the west so many years ago. His anticipated

speaking tour, however, turned out to be something other than
what the Québec nationalists had hoped. Dumont was simply
too honest a man. He did not embellish his stories with the
colourful political rhetoric that his sponsors used and abused
to play to the crowds. He simply endeavoured to tell the truth
as he remembered it—an approach that led to an embarrassing
complication for the nationalists. Dumont had always believed
that the Roman Catholic clergy in the Batoche area had betrayed
the Métis. He publicly recalled the priests' confession to the
devout Métis warriors and their families before battle. He voiced
his suspicion that the priests who crossed over to the Canadian
side had informed Middleton about the Métis' military status
and strategy.

Dumont was not afraid to dwell on the stance of the
Saskatchewan clergy to his wholly French Roman Catholic audiences. Not that the audiences were large, for it was while Gabriel
lectured in Québec that he learned of public apathy and forget-
fulness. It had been three years since the dramatic flame of
rebellion had flared up in the North-West, and while some were
still interested, the relentless pressure of current events had
begun to mercilessly sweep the rebellion into the pages of history. As word of Dumont's occasional anti-clerical indiscretions
spread, his talks were quickly transformed from well-attended
curiosities into sparsely attended embarrassments. The Québec
nationalists prematurely removed their sponsorship, and the
speaking tour quietly ground to an early halt.

Dumont resumed one last period of wandering. In the summer of 1888, he travelled around Montana, Dakota and even
ventured into Red River country, although he had yet to find it in
his heart to return to Batoche. Here, too, things were changing, as
the memory of the rebellion slipped into the past a little more
every day. A homeless and restless Dumont returned to Québec
and took up briefly with a group of Québec intellectuals and

journalists. Dumont would eventually dictate the first of his two accounts of the North-West Rebellion to these men.

In the spring of 1889, Gabriel booked passage on a ship and left the continent for the first time in his life to spend a year in Paris. Little is known of his trip to France; he spoke of it rarely and briefly when asked—an uncharacteristic reticence suggesting that the foreign shores of France proved less than entrancing to the rugged plainsmen. And while Dumont still did not feel ready to return to the bosom of the prairie that had reared him, he would never again venture so far from his country.

He returned to the Métis settlements of Montana in 1890, where one last life and death struggle awaited him. It happened on a group hunting expedition, at night, while Gabriel slept in his tent. A sharp pain that shot across his head rudely awakened Dumont. A man standing above him had stabbed him in the head, and the knife blow glanced off his tough skull, slicing through the skin behind his left ear. While a younger Gabriel Dumont would probably have never allowed an enemy to get that close to him in his sleep, the old warrior, now over 50 years old, reacted to the attack with the same speed he would have in his prime. Dumont jumped up and threw off his would-be assassin in one powerful motion. He could faintly make out the man's features in the faint light, enough to know that he had never seen the man before.

"What do you want?" Gabriel asked, as he shifted his weight to receive another attack.

His assailant lunged for him again, leading with a large gleaming knife in his right hand. A fierce fight ensued, in which Dumont's strong opponent managed to keep his knife hand free and stab Dumont several times in the back and the stomach. As the stranger cut his long bloody swaths, Dumont bit his lip to contain the shouts of pain. But the old buffalo hunter still had a few tricks up his sleeve. Employing a little frontier judo, Dumont flipped his attacker onto his back and promptly brought his full weight to bear, crushing the man's shoulders down with his knees and ramming his fist down his would-be assassin's throat. The man brought his knife up to Gabriel's neck, but Dumont grabbed it by the blade, cutting his fingers to the bone, but still managing to yank it out of the man's hands.

The fight ended when the men from the surrounding tents, finally awakened by the sounds of the fight, stormed in and pulled the Métis patriarch off the assassin. It took every man there to tear Gabriel away from the fight, thus allowing the attacker to dash from the tent. The man got away, leaving his pursuers in the dark and his identity forever a mystery. No one could say who he was or what his motivation might have been, but Dumont always maintained that he was an assassin hired by the Canadian government.

In 1893, after a little more wandering and a few more efforts to raise money in Québec for the still-impoverished Métis of the Saskatchewan valley, Dumont finally returned home. He rode slowly past the charred and crumbling remains of the home that he and Madeleine had shared for so many years, the sound of his horse's hooves on the prairie stirring old embers and memories. He visited with friends and family members whom he had not seen in more than eight years. He tried to have his land title officially recognized and experienced for himself the bureaucratic delays and difficulties that his Métis people were enduring at the hands of the government.

Dumont, at 56 years old, had never been more than a perfunctory farmer, and he found that he still could not seriously pursue that sedentary lifestyle upon his return. Instead, he settled in on the homestead of his beloved nephew, Alexis—the same nephew who had run through the roving patrols of Canadian soldiers to deliver food and parting words to his uncle after the Battle of Batoche. Dumont built a modest cabin for himself and began to enjoy being among his own people again.

Gabriel Dumont, age 63, taken in 1900

He visited with old friends and long-since-forgiven former enemies, even resuming his friendship with Charles Nolin, who invited the ageing Gabriel to live in his house. Dumont declined. Gabriel and the events in which he had played such a leading role were the stuff of legend in this country, and people sought him out to hear him tell his tales of Crozier, Middleton and Riel.

Gabriel Dumont's gravesite in Batoche, Saskatchewan

And it was on a slightly more formal and organized occasion in 1903, that Dumont gave his second and final recorded account of the North-West Rebellion.

He was 61 years old but still active, and he continued to travel to Montana and Dakota, even occasionally appearing on the streets of Winnipeg. To provide for himself, Dumont continued to hunt. He would always give some of the meat from his hunting expeditions to Alexis and his family, thankful for their kindness and happy to be able to contribute something in return.

After a hunting trip to Basin Lake in mid-May 1906, Dumont returned complaining to his nephew of sharp pains in his arms and chest. For the next few days, Gabriel continued with his normal activities: he went for brisk walks through the rural community and engaged in conversation with friends just as eagerly. The pain did not go away, but Gabriel would have shrugged it off, perhaps assuming that he had just pulled a muscle. If he did make such an assumption, he was wrong. On Saturday, May 14, Alexis' wife poured her uncle a bowl of hearty soup as he came in the door after one of his walks. Gabriel sat down briefly, had a few mouthfuls, silently stood up, made his way over to the nearest bed and collapsed, dead.

He died in 1906 outliving his adversaries John A. Macdonald (1891), Frederick Middleton (1898), and Lief Crozier (1901). Gabriel Dumont's body was laid to rest in the Batoche cemetery among the graves of so many Métis who had fought under him during the 1885 rebellion. And fittingly, as the assembled Métis listened to Father Moulin give the funeral oration over his old friend's body, they were able to look around from the hilltop and out over the general's final battlefield.

Notes on Sources

Beal, Bob & Rod Macleod. *Praire Fire: The 1885 North-West Rebellion*. Edmonton: Hurtig, 1984.

Boulton, C. A. *Reminiscences of the North-West Rebellions*. Ottawa: National Library of Canada, 1976.

Charette, Guillaume. *Vanishing Spaces: The Memoirs of Prairie Métis*. Winnipeg: Bois-Brulés. 1980.

Dumont, Gabriel, translated by Michael Barnholden. *Gabriel Dumont Speaks*. Vancouver, BC: Talonbooks, 1993.

Flanagan, Thomas (ed.). *The Diaries of Louis Riel*. Edmonton: Hurtig. 1976.

Howard, Joseph Kinsey, *Strange Empire: The Story of Louis Riel*. Toronto: Swan Publishing, 1952.

McKee, Sandra Lynn. *Canadian Plainsmen: Gabriel Dumont, Jerry Potts*. Surrey: Heritage House Publishing, 1982.

———. *Gabriel Dumont, Indian Fighter*. Frontiers Unlimited, 1967.

Morton, Desmond. *The Last War Drum: The North-West Campaign of 1885*. Toronto: Hakkert, 1972.

Siggins, Maggie. *Riel: A Life of Revolution.* Toronto: Harper-Collins. 1994.

Sissons, C. K. *John Kerr.* Ottawa: National Library of Canada. 1977.

Stanley, G. F. G. "Gabriel Dumont's Account of the North-West Rebellion, 1885." *Canadian Historical* Review. 1949

Woodcock, George. *Gabriel Dumont: The Métis Chief and his Lost World.* Peterborough: Broadview Press, 2003.

About the Authors

Dan Asfar is no stranger to fans of narrative histories about the American and Canadian West. Driven by a love of history and a passion for dramatic narration, Dan has written two other popular history volumes: *Louis Riel* and *Outlaws and Lawmen of the West: Volume II.*

This is Tim Chodan second book with Dan Asfar. *Louis Riel* was the first. He has a lifelong interest in Canadian history and is a skilled researcher.

Together the two have written two compelling biographies: the first of Louis Riel, who rallied the Red River Métis against the Canadian government over Métis rights and land in the Red River Resistance and the 1885 North-West Rebellion; and the second about Gabriel Dumont, Riel's mighty general who led the Métis of the Saskatchewan valley to secure their own rights and land in what would become the new province of Saskatchewan.

Sitting Bull in Canada
by Tony Hollihan

This book recounts the story of Sioux chief Sitting Bull's retreat into Canada after the Battle of the Little Bighorn. The story centers on the friendship that developed between the fierce warrior and the celebrated Mountie Major James Walsh.

$10.95 US • $14.95 CDN • ISBN 1-894864-02-6
5.25" x 8.25" • 288 pages

Great Chiefs, Volume I
by Tony Hollihan

Chronicled here are the lives of famous Native chiefs and warriors who grappled with the increasing encroachment of European settlers in the West. The author dynamically brings to life these remarkable leaders and the means they adopted in a desperate bid to protect their people. Sitting Bull, Chief Joseph, Quanah Parker, Red Cloud, Louis Riel and Sequoyah are featured.

$10.95 US • $14.95 CDN • ISBN 1-894864-03-4
5.25" x 8.25" • 320 pages

Great Chiefs, Volume II
by Tony Hollihan

Tony Hollihan weaves more spellbinding tales of the courageous chiefs and warriors of North America's western tribes who battled valiantly against the growing tide of European settlement on their ancestral lands. Geronimo, Tecumseh, Crowfoot, Plenty Coups, Wovoka and Crazy Horse are featured.

$10.95 US • $14.95 CDN • ISBN 1-894864-07-7
5.25" x 8.25" • 320 pages

Look for books in the *Legends* series at your local bookseller and newsstand or contact the distributor, Lone Pine Publishing, directly. In the U.S. call 1-800-518-3541. In Canada, call 1-800-661-9017.